"*Life for the Academic in the Neoliberal University* is a ground breaking book. It not only details with great rigor and clarity how higher education has become an outpost of neoliberal violence, it also points to how it has created an existential crisis for those faculty, students, and others who believe that the university has an obligation to cultivate those capacities, forms of knowledge, and values that deepen and extend the practice of freedom essential to any democracy. This book should be read by everyone who refuses to give up on higher education while recognizing the need to struggle over its most democratic possibilities."

Henry Giroux
McMaster University Professor for Scholarship in the Public Interest
The Paulo Freire Distinguished Scholar in Critical Pedagogy
Author of Neoliberalism's War on Higher Education

"Higher education is now lived as an experience of neoliberalism. This book explores these experiences and changes and the damage they do to academics, and the university itself, which has become a key site of neoliberalism. *Life for the Academic in the Neoliberal University* is a chilling read but important because the critical analysis is dire but the alternatives presented are optimistic."

Stephen J Ball FBA
Distinguished Service Professor of Sociology of Education,
Institute of Education, University College London
Author of The Education Debate

"*Life for the Academic in the Neoliberal University* grounds critique of the everyday experiences of academics and students against the structures of neoliberal control that demand toxic performance management. Alpesh Maisuria and Enja Helmes present a dialectical engagement between theory and concrete, lived experiences grounded in the humanities and social sciences, in order to critique the economistic obsession with human capital that demands competition in the construction of specific academic-types. In addressing the impact on mental health and the generation of ill-being across universities, the authors challenge us to reconsider the potential for alternative structures, governance and regulation surrounding higher education. The book culminates with a provocative argument for a National Education Service (NES) based on co-operative principles and practices, which should ignite much needed discussion and action. As a result, this is an important book in addressing the potential for the democratic production of the University infused with a humanist tradition."

Richard Hall
Professor of Education and Technology, De Montfort University,
and National Teaching Fellow
Author of The Alienated Academic: The Struggle for
Autonomy Inside the University

Life for the Academic in the Neoliberal University

Life for the Academic in the Neoliberal University investigates the impact of neoliberalism on academics in today's universities. Considering the experiences of early career researchers as well as more experienced academics, it outlines the changing nature of working life in the university precipitated by the reality of de-professionalisation, worsening conditions of employment, and general precarious existence.

The book traces the dramatic shift in the role and function of universities and academics over the last forty years. It considers how capitalist neoliberalism drives universities to operate like businesses in a cut-throat financialised education market place. Uniquely the book then provides a possible alternative in the form of the National Education Service (NES) and what this alternative system could look like.

Thought-provoking and relevant, this book will be of useful to postgraduate students as well as new, emerging, and established academics interested in the current state of higher education, academic life, and possibilities for the future.

Alpesh Maisuria is a senior lecturer in Education Studies at the University of East London, UK.

Svenja Helmes is a researcher at the University of Sheffield, UK.

Routledge Research in Higher Education

The Phenomenological Heart of Teaching and Learning
Theory, Research, and Practice in Higher Education
*Katherine H. Greenberg, Brian K. Sohn, Neil B. Greenberg,
Howard R. Pollio, Sandra P. Thomas, and John T. Smith*

The Tenure-Track Process for Chicana and Latina Faculty
Experiences of Resisting and Persisting in the Academy
Edited by Patricia A. Pérez

Higher Education in Nepal
Policies and Perspectives
Edited by Krishna Bista, Shyam Sharma, and Rosalind Latiner Raby

Race, Law, and Higher Education in the Colorblind Era
Critical Investigations into Race-Related Supreme Court Disputes
Hoang Vu Tran

Post-Recession Community College Reform
A Decade of Experimentation
Chet Jordan and Anthony G. Picciano

Building Soft Skills for Employability
Challenges and Practices in Vietnam
Tran Le Huu Nghia

Life for the Academic in the Neoliberal University
Alpesh Maisuria and Svenja Helmes

For more information about this series, please visit: www.routledge.com/
Routledge-Research-in-Higher-Education/book-series/RRHE

Life for the Academic in the Neoliberal University

Alpesh Maisuria and Svenja Helmes

FOREWORD BY PETER McLAREN

LONDON AND NEW YORK

First published 2020
by Routledge
2 Park Square, Milton Park, Abingdon, Oxon OX14 4RN
and by Routledge
52 Vanderbilt Avenue, New York, NY 10017

Routledge is an imprint of the Taylor & Francis Group, an informa business

First issued in paperback 2021

© 2020 Alpesh Maisuria and Svenja Helmes

The right of Alpesh Maisuria and Svenja Helmes to be identified as authors of this work has been asserted by them in accordance with sections 77 and 78 of the Copyright, Designs and Patents Act 1988.

All rights reserved. No part of this book may be reprinted or reproduced or utilised in any form or by any electronic, mechanical, or other means, now known or hereafter invented, including photocopying and recording, or in any information storage or retrieval system, without permission in writing from the publishers.

Trademark notice: Product or corporate names may be trademarks or registered trademarks, and are used only for identification and explanation without intent to infringe.

British Library Cataloguing-in-Publication Data
A catalogue record for this book is available from the British Library

Library of Congress Cataloging-in-Publication Data
A catalog record has been requested for this book

ISBN: 978-0-367-34768-0 (hbk)
ISBN: 978-1-03-208869-3 (pbk)
ISBN: 978-0-429-32995-1 (ebk)

Typeset in Galliard
by codeMantra

For Archie, Oscar & Jo
For Papa & Peter

Contents

Foreword	xi
Preface	xix
Organisation of the book	xxi

1 **The neoliberal capitalist system and education**   1
   Origins of capitalism 1
   Neoliberal turn 7
   *Higher education for creating labour and
      productivity 8*
   Knowledge economy 11

2 **Neoliberalisation of the university and
   academic work**   15
   Competition and (Quasi-)privatisation 15
   Technology 23
   The competitive academic 25
   Curriculum 30

3 **Reality for new and prospective academics, and
   postgraduate students**   34
   *Flexibility, transferable skills and the social sciences/
      humanities 34*
   Targets and mental health 39
   Early career academics 45

4 **Struggle for a new reality**   52
   Feasibility of the emergence of alternatives 52

x   Contents

   Towards the National Education Service (NES) 54
   Alternative universities 63

References 73
Index 85

Foreword

Like many who chose a life in the academy, I was a youthful adventurer committed to provide ballast for headstrong students of critical consciousness. But that spirit of discovery that infused my early days as an academic soon became tempered, if not overmastered, prone to being capsized in the ribald currents of university life. It is now an academic life no longer bound by earlier commitments to ensuring professional autonomy, academic freedom, and a search for ways of providing a new stewardship for a planet now rotting before our downcast eyes. In other domains of social and political life, they would describe this state of affairs as a historical betrayal of trust, but today in colleges and universities it's referred to as 'practical', as if the arc of history compels itself on its own to take the path most profitable for the mandarins of finance and only slowly, haltingly and hesitatingly does it concern itself with other trajectories – such as a robust engagement with the epistemologies, ontologies, and ethics of knowing.

It is with this reflection that I write the following warning about neoliberalism for academics across the pond, whose academy is following us in the US.

Here, plump university endowments are used to invest in expanding neoliberalism in universities. Rarely are they used to provide a living wage for those who do most of the heavy lifting – teaching students, grading papers, organising tutorials, etc. The metrics by which we now judge a successful university are the utility of those selfsame metrics – which unsurprisingly is in concert with the reigning paradigm of capitalist growth. That the gold standard of today's neoliberal university is the efficacy of its metrics should come as no surprise to those who have not lost their taste for thinking critically – and how many standard deviations from the norm this represents I shall leave to the accountants and consultants who run the universities to figure out in front of their computers. Critical education for social justice, unsullied by administrative clerics and untouched by the redactors-in-chiefs, and presented to the public in its raw contempt for helping to reproduce the worst elements of the society of the spectacle, is attacked through a *sola economicus* hermeneutic and socialist straw man, bolstered by conceptual "swag attire" from the *Wall Street Journal* – the sartorial equivalent of wearing a pair of $6,000 Yeezys along with your cap and gown. If you wish to attend soirees with Conrad Black-type mountebanks or thrill in the mysteries of Yale's Skull and Bones secret society, or engage in golden showers with Russian oligarchs and orange-haired tyrants, then presumably you already have the financial means to reach your goal. This tarnishes the claim that education remains in the pursuit of freedom and social justice. Today, becoming educated in the vaulted halls of higher learning means little if it can't help your capital investment augment value, enhance through public exposition your personal brand, and help you purchase a house in the Hamptons. Education is big business and if you don't believe that, then follow the money. When the prestigious Rossier School of Education at the University of Southern California developed their online Masters of Arts in Teaching programme, colleagues of mine scoffed but within several years it had several thousand students paying full tuition with a full online degree and remote sites for student teaching. Their reputation as an elite university prevailed even as it sold its soul and it went on to make a fortune, continuing to this day. Stagnating wages and decreased benefits that have been more or less constant since the 1970s constitute a major problem in our age of austerity capitalism, especially as public services and welfare are shrinking across the country. And what a challenge this has become for social justice educators! Some scientists today are warning humanity that we have entered the sixth period of extinction which began in 2010. The massive emission of carbon dioxide from fossil fuels is implicating many life forms on Earth – and not for the best. And this will intensify over the next three to four decades. And while our biosphere continues to rot, another stench engulfs us, this time ideological. Notorious paleo-conservatives – mentors of the likes of Steve Bannon such as William Lind – announce that we have entered a period of fourth-generation warfare that includes cyber-attacks involving decentralised media networks, low-intensity conflicts such as "culture wars" (i.e. political correctness, feminism, multiculturalism, and immigration) and guerrilla strategies and tactics directed towards the surveillance state. Such situations present a harrowing backdrop for the remaining drama of the struggle for human civilization. Critical theorists in the US influenced by Frankfurt School intellectuals are being held responsible for the breakdown of the US Judeo-Christian values – which includes most if not all of us involved in critical pedagogy. There is a lot of work to be done, and we won't be able to carry this work out as long as we are being trained in college and universities to become spineless clerks of the empire. We have entered an age of dogma, in which the nuances of reason have been sacrificed to the iron-fisted rhetoric of persuasion through a politics of authoritarianism, all of which can be traced to the social relations of capitalist production, the financialisation of the economy, attacks on unions, floating exchange rates, shock doctrine politics, austerity capitalism, racism, white supremacy, homophobia, patriarchy: neoliberalism's usual suspects.

Throughout my 30 years in the university, I have taught doctoral students who have had to work in strip clubs, who lived in their cars, who slept in alleys, who were escaping a harrowing existence on the streets of Los Angeles. Those were considered unusual circumstances for those of us fortunate enough to be among the professoriate, luxuriating in our swivel chairs and expounding to our students and peers in faux-Oxbridge offices in the outskirts of Silicon Valley. Now, at a time when government funding for public universities is falling, when the "businessification" of universities has become the new normal, there are increasing numbers of freshly minted graduates from respected doctoral programmes who are being hired to teach single courses. Also included in this precarious situation are more experienced adjunct professors who have been seeking three-year contracts and who are similarly scraping by, utilising any means that they can to pay off student debt, to find food and shelter and to publish some articles so as to increase their chances of finding the mother load – a tenure-track position. Some are enrolled in public assistance programmes, eat at food banks, some turn to sex work, and some are homeless. A report by Alastair Gee (2017) in *The Guardian* includes the following description:

> Sex work is one of the more unusual ways that adjuncts have avoided living in poverty, and perhaps even homelessness. A quarter of part-time college academics (many of whom are adjuncts, though it's not uncommon for adjuncts to work 40 hours a week or more) are said to be enrolled in public assistance programmes such as Medicaid.

They resort to food banks and Goodwill, and there is even an adjuncts' cookbook that shows how to turn items like beef scraps, chicken bones, and orange peel into meals. And then there are those who are either on the streets or teetering on the edge of losing stable housing.

Even highly successful adjuncts who are able to secure six courses per year and put in 60-hour weeks are lucky to earn $40,000 a year whereas the median income for adjuncts is approximately $22,041 a year. Full-time faculty earn approximately $47,500 (Gee, 2017). And private institutions?

According to Gee (2017):

> Adjuncting has grown as funding for public universities has fallen by more than a quarter between 1990 and 2009. Private institutions also recognize the allure of part-time professors: generally, they are cheaper than full-time staff, don't receive benefits or support for their personal research, and their hours can be carefully limited so they do not teach enough to qualify for health insurance.

The sheer numbers of precarious academic workers put the lie to the notion that all the hard work of earning a doctorate and the passion for research and teaching will pay off when those carved oak doors of the academy swing open, offering a portal to a world rich in opportunities to contribute to the public good as well as to acquire the creature comforts of a middle-class existence. It's more likely that adjunct work will force you and your family to rely on food stamps, the Children's Health Insurance Program, cash welfare, the Supplemental Nutrition Assistance Program, or the Earned Income Tax Credit. Long past are the days of the polished mahogany desk decorated with a brass inkwell, hand-carved pipe stands, arcane artefacts collected during talks abroad, and heaps of well-thumbed books with covers carefully angled towards the door to impress visiting colleagues eager to collaborate in your important research projects. Today you are lucky to teach two or three classes per semester and don't have to re-mortgage your house, rent out the spare bedroom, or add your name to the growing lists for government-subsidized housing. I have a friend who teaches as an adjunct and lives in a tent in the woods – fortunately the climate in southern California will not be overly punishing in this regard. Adjuncts have made some gains by unionizing, but much work needs to be done.

At a time when Hollywood celebrities and private equity executives spend a fortune in bribes to get their children into elite schools, what does that say for the working-poor who were promised by the guiding narrative of meritocracy that their hard work would give them a chance to enter the country's best colleges. According to Kevin Carey (2019), these colleges constitute 'an overpriced gated community whose benefits accrue mostly to the wealthy. At 38 colleges, including Yale, Princeton, Brown and Penn, there are more students from the top 1 percent than the bottom 60 percent'. Carey writes:

> Tuition prices aren't the only reason for this, but they're a major one. Public university tuition has doubled in the last two decades, tripled in the last three. Prestige-hungry universities admit large numbers of

students who can pay ever-increasing fees and only a relative handful of low-income students. The US now has more student loan debt than credit card debt – upward of $1.5 trillion. Nearly 40 percent of borrowers who entered college in the 2003 academic year could default on their loans by 2023, the Brookings Institution predicts.

Online courses, you would think, could be a more cost-effective means of educating students unable or unwilling to shoulder a student debt that is the equivalent of a modest home mortgage. Such a course offering "could break the tuition cost curve by making the price of online degrees proportional to what colleges actually spend to operate the courses" (Carey, 2019). But the stark reality is that they don't, as they are reluctant "to pass even the tiniest fraction of the savings on to students. They charge online students the same astronomical prices they levy for the on-campus experience" (Carey, 2019) since they hire expensive private companies – OPMs (Online Program Managers) – to help run their online degrees, companies that take approximately 60 percent of the tuition fees.

According to Carey (2019), these companies:

> Outsource much of the work to an obscure species of for-profit company that has figured out how to gouge students in new and creative ways. These companies are called online program managers, or OPMs, an acronym that could come right out of "Office Space". They have goofy, forgettable names like 2U, HotChalk, and iDesign. As the founder of 2U puts it, 'The more invisible we are, the better'.

But OPMs are transforming both the economics and the practice of higher learning. They help a growing number of America's most-lauded colleges provide online degrees – including Harvard, Yale, Georgetown, NYU, UC Berkeley, UNC Chapel Hill, Northwestern, Syracuse, Rice, and USC, to name just a few. The schools often omit any mention of these companies on their course pages, but OPMs typically take a 60 percent cut of tuition, sometimes more. Trace Urdan, managing director at the investment bank and consulting firm Tyton Partners, estimates that the market for OPMs and related services will be worth nearly $8 billion by 2020.

Carey (2019) sums up the neoliberal rationale of education in these times:

> What this means is that an innovation that should have been used to address inequality is serving to fuel it. Instead of students receiving a reasonably priced, quality online degree, universities are using them as cash cows while corporate middlemen hoover up the greater share of

the profits. In a perfect twist, big tech companies are getting the spill-off, in the form of massive sums spent on Facebook and Google ads. It's a near-perfect encapsulation of the social and structural forces that allow the already-rich to get richer at the expense of everyone else.

The big cash cows are master's degrees. They are part of a criminal enterprise, run by the academic equivalent of Chicago's old mafia dons:

Colleges are legally required to publicly report undergraduate admissions statistics, including SAT scores and what percentage of their applicants gain admission. This prevents elite schools from simply jacking up the number of students admitted to their most prestigious undergraduate programmes to make more money – those programmes are sought after precisely because they are exclusive. Ph.D. programmes at elite universities tend to be similarly selective.

By contrast, master's programmes are a black box – there is no requirement to publish any admissions data. This means universities can dramatically lower their admissions standards and enrol thousands of highly profitable students without sullying their brand. The University of Pennsylvania, for example, offers a master's in "Applied Positive Psychology," which is essentially a $66,000 Ivy League degree in self-affirmation. It has "no specific prerequisite courses" and applications are accepted from anyone with a minimum 3.0 grade point average. According to a UPenn official, the programme, which launched 15 years ago, is for individuals who 'desire to apply evidence-based positive psychology to their area of expertise' (Carey, 2019).

As long as a master's degree is accredited, there are no limits to what a student can borrow. In fact, students are eligible for federal loans for the entire cost of tuition, fees, books, and living expenses, often in excess of $100,000. And there is no limit on what the college can charge.

This makes us wonder if there are goals to education under the Wehrmacht of neoliberalism other than profit-making for the universities? But what about the actual conditions faced by education workers inside the walls of our once-hallowed institutions?

While there are identifiable similarities to the neoliberalising currents implicating the lives of university workers in the US, university life in the UK faces its own localised challenges. These challenges are analysed in this new volume by Maisuria and Helmes. They meticulously undress the swindle of fulfilment surrounding education, exposing the sham hiding behind the ideological and economic curtains of our neoliberal theatre of academic operations. The values reaffirmed in the *Magna Charta Universitatum* in 1988 (Banfield, Maisuria, and Raduntz, 2016) have, according to Maisuria and Helmes, been lost to history, floating like dregs through the sewers of those neoliberal agencies that are responsible for credentialising our identities – for creating our own person brand and polishing our uniquely neoliberal 'skill sets' – as worthy instruments of the corporate will in the great crusade to become the new Knights Templar of commodity production. The nature of academic work and the purpose of the university itself under the guardians of neoliberalism must be held up to scrutiny. This is especially the case for social justice educators who define education very differently from those policing and running universities, whose obsession with employability metrics scuttles entire philosophy departments in order to bolster, say, biochemistry. Julian Baggini (2018) reports:

> You might think that a university philosophy department facing closure in Hull is of as much interest to the average person as the shutting of a butcher's in Wolverhampton is to a vegetarian in Totnes. There are almost as many universities as high streets now, and for every closure here there's an opening somewhere else. But the events unfolding on Humberside are symptomatic of a deep malaise affecting not just universities but the wider culture. The crude pursuit of what is "practical", "efficient" or "useful" is threatening everything of value that isn't evidently profitable.

For many philosophers, the major goals of education are bound up with the task of linking scholarship to the moral and political imperatives of social justice. But this requires a space of learning where ideational kinetic energy necessary for critical inquiry can be produced without needless obstruction or obfuscation, without falling into what Paulo Freire called "bureaucratization of mind" (1985, p 15). That the voices of education workers fail to be incorporated into decision-making over the nature of working conditions has sadly become one of the truisms of our educational times.

Very often critical educators must resort to a coded language with their students, to avoid the 'quality' controlling eye of the Dean, the Rector, or the Chair. As someone who has hung out with academic comrades in London pubs, I've listened to many of their experiences – excruciatingly depressing – resulting from championing with unwavering zeal the works of a philosopher nicknamed the "Old Moor". And I had my own stories to share. For example, in 2006 I was placed on top of a list of 30 "dangerous" professors at UCLA, and the organisation responsible for the list offered to pay students 100 dollars to secretly audiotape my classes and 50 dollars to provide notes from my lectures. One of my crimes was working in Venezuela on behalf of the Bolivarian revolution, offering what advice I could to create opportunities for a socialist education. Venezuela has its share of important educators who have left their mark on history, such as Simón Rodríguez, tutor and mentor to Simón Bolívar, and during my time there I was educated by the *campesinos*, who became my teachers.

This book successfully explicates the impact of neoliberalism on the life of increasingly alienated academic workers and offers an unsparing analysis of the likely conditions they will face in the foreseeable future in England, like the one I have accounted above in the US. Universities continue to grow profits, but such growth is decoupled from the wages and better working conditions for the academics whose labour power fuels such growth. The authors make clear that any possible exit from this situation must have as a priority a critique of political economy and viable alternatives, such as the National Education Service, for a better world.

Peter McLaren is Distinguished Professor in Critical Studies, College of Educational Studies, Chapman University, where he is Co-Director of the Paulo Freire Democratic Project and International Ambassador for Global Ethics and Social Justice.

Preface

'We're f*****, it's over, I'm done with this'. This was the way a newly appointed academic colleague recently expressed his assessment of life in his university. The deep frustration with which he delivered his remarks and sadness-tinged desire to exit academia are increasingly common sentiments amongst academics in England and beyond. While each university has their own institutional mission statements and objectives, the common thread that pulls them together is the structural conditions imposed by neoliberalism that are lived by academics.

Universities are in a rapidly neoliberalising environment, and in this there are significant changes to their nature and purpose, and what academics do. The detrimental reality of these changes has been painfully reported in *The Guardian* Newspaper blog *Academics Anonymous* (AA), which has served as an outlet to expose working conditions in universities in England. Generally, the consensus among academics is that universities in these neoliberal times are no longer reflective of traditional values contained as part of the history of the development of the university, and these values were reaffirmed in vain by the *Magna Charta Universitatum* in 1988 (Banfield, Maisuria, and Raduntz, 2016). The zeitgeist of these values was that the nature and purpose of universities ought to be bound up with fundamental principles of autonomy and freedom, and that this was a moral as well as an intellectual endeavour. The reality now is very different. According to Collini (2018), 'viewed from the everyday experience of a British university... these principles can ring hollow'. This apparent hollowing-out of autonomy and freedom fundamentally changes the role and function of the university academic, thus problematising the nature of academic work and the purpose of the university itself in neoliberalism.

According to most academics in the social sciences and humanities, the question that pervades is: what remains of the spaces to do critical, cultural, and creative work when what is extrinsically valued and institutionally supported is performance and outputs for league tables, student recruitment, employability metrics, and contribution to economic productivity. As we show, there are serious consequences for the maverick academic who dares to veer away from these, coercing even the most Marxist to play the metrics, outputs, and performativity game – this book could be considered as an example. As Tony Green said, capitalism makes fools of us all (Green, 2007).

The arguments are a treatment of the English higher education system, but they resonate globally where neoliberalism exists. Written in an accessible fashion without losing the nuanced and sophisticated nature of the debate, through a critical lens this book aims to explicate the impact of neoliberalism on the life of most academics in most mainstream universities and their increasingly complex and even compromised position in neoliberalism. Uniquely, we include discussion relating to the conditions for new and prospective academics in this landscape, including an important discussion of actual experiences and mental health in a restrictive performativity culture. We finish the book with optimism, evaluating two alternative universities, and provide argument and suggestions in support of the creation of the National Education Service as a progressive initiative to build the momentum to fight against the dismal existence and dire future of education in neoliberalism.

Organisation of the book

We have divided the book into four chapters that are individually distinct and also sequential. As a result, the book can be read as totality or the reader may wish to dip into specific chapters of interest.

In Chapter 1, *The neoliberal capitalist system and education*, we begin by providing a brief introduction and summary of capitalism and its latest stage – neoliberalism. We do not intend this to be a comprehensive descriptive analysis, but our entire discussion and argument is underpinned by critique of neoliberal ideology, practice, and political economy, and so for clarity it is incumbent on us to provide something about what we mean by its use (c.f. Maisuria and Cole, 2017). After this, we can then focus on the ways in which the university has been reconfigured to be more like, and also serving, for-profit corporations (Ryan, 2017). Specifically explicated is how universities have been subsumed into the needs of the economy and everything else is secondary (Maisuria and Cole, 2017). This means universities, as publicly funded organisations, must create labour capacity to fuel neoliberalism and industrial productivity, which we explain is part of the financialisation of higher education. We engage in a discussion about the creation of the *knowledge economy* which brings a neoliberal role and function to universities, all of this moves education away from being a public service.

In Chapter 2 – *Neoliberalisation of the university and academic work*, we commence with exploring the inherent competition within and between universities, and also their (*Quasi-*)*privatisation*. We account for the ways in which marketisation seems now to be a core of university business (Hill et al., 2015). We aim to show that reputation and corporate branding drive what is valued, over and above teaching, learning, and research, which is based on creative and critical thinking. Secondly, we focus on the role of *technology*. Technology has often been promoted as being a driver of innovation, but in the neoliberal university it is increasingly deployed for different and nefarious purposes, including surveillance of the academic's work and practices, as part of performance management. Technology is also used for cost-saving by eliminating the need for face-to-face teaching and learning; concern for the quality of the student experience becomes marketing rhetoric. In the third section, we explore the role of *the competitive academic* and how competition negatively coerces academic life. In the current era of neoliberal capitalism, competition is a crucial element of the nature of academia that academics are coerced to acquiesce with. We relate these working conditions to the idea of class struggle, and argue that academics, despite their qualifications and social status, are vulnerable and precarious labourers. Not only can academics be relatively easily replaced by cheaper labour (hourly paid juniors) or technology, but their role has also become one that is focused on applying for research funding and publishing work that can generate money and marketable reputation. This is far removed from the *Magna Charta Universitatum*. In the final discussion of this chapter, we look at the *curriculum* offering in HE and the ways that it has shifted from being critical, creative, and holistic – to one that is increasingly restricting its remit to prioritise employability and a narrow-financialised conception of entrepreneurialism. We expose this shift as a hidden as well as overt consequence of neoliberalism.

In the third chapter, **Reality for new and prospective academics, and postgraduate students**, we elaborate on the previous chapters by focusing on the consequences of the neoliberal shifts and changes to the postgraduate student and new lecturer experience. Importantly, the postgraduate is the next generation of academic, therefore we examine the possibility of doing creative and critical work in conditions where neoliberal marketability and metrics are prioritised. The neoliberal managerial buzzword – *resilience* – is used as a framing device for this discussion. We argue that a promotion of resilience enables increased exploitation and alienation, and a more-for-less culture. *Resilience* comes with the necessity for the academic to be flexible and striving (words such as stretch objectives appear in performativity reviews). In practice, this is about working in a competitive environment where one must be seen to be doing more hours, for new and prospective academics this translates to more teaching and administration, and for more established academics this is about producing ever more outputs and increasingly larger research grant capture. Research outputs are part of an expanding metrics and datafication culture, which we discuss using the concept of *performativity*. In this section, we draw on *The Guardian* newspaper's *Academics Anonymous* blog to provide testimony for our discussions. Building on previous sections of this chapter where the experiences of GTAs and prospective academics were explored, the final section focuses more extensively on the experiences of those who have just entered the profession as new academics, in literature often described as early career academics (ECAs). We explore their position within the university, the ethical dilemmas they face when entering a system that seeks to restrict their autonomy and stifle their creativity, and their quest for establishing an academic identity.

In the final chapter, *Struggle for a new reality*, we broaden the discussion and speculate on an alternative vision of higher education and the nature of academic work in this. We begin with a theoretical discussion, drawing from Antonio Gramsci, to frame the argument for the National Education Service (NES) with the concept of feasibility. We state the necessity of academics and others to view the possibility being open for a different kind of education system, structure, and experience to come into existence. We then go on to describe the proposal for the NES, which the chapter is dedicated to advancing as a progressive move to build the impetus for challenging neoliberalism itself. We outline principles and practices that should underpin a future nationalised and non-neoliberal higher education sector. We then elaborate on existing attempts at creating an alternative free university using the case study of the Social Science Centre (SSC) in Lincoln and Manchester. Both of these ultimately succumbed to neoliberal and financial pressures, and the newest creation is the Co-operative University due to open soon, but different from the SSC, charging £5,500. We argue that a nationalised and non-neoliberal higher education sector as part of the NES could incorporate and mainstream, a free education based on co-operative principles – this is the provocation of the book.

1 The neoliberal capitalist system and education

Origins of capitalism

Since its emergence in the 1600s, capitalism has been subjected to much discussion about its role in human life within a range of contexts, especially about social justice, equality, and equity. More recently and especially in relation to Thatcherism and Reaganism, it has also been discussed in relation to education (Maisuria, 2015), and there has been a proliferation of scholarship and commentary over recent decades. A very brief sketching of relevant history for pinning the analysis in this book is a useful point of departure.

Capitalism can be traced back to at least the early days of colonisation where expanding ownership of private property (land, resources, and human slaves) was of primary concern for the ruling class who had their sights on empire-building for the purposes of wealth, power, and capital accumulation (Bowles and Gintis, 1976). This was all part of a historic struggle, and in Europe it took 'half a millennium of conflict and piecemeal change' (ibid., p. 58). Regardless of where and at what pace, the expansion of the capitalist system required increasingly exploitable labour power to be increasingly productive in generating and accumulating capital. Karl Marx was the first to claim capitalism as being about a mode of production (Marx, 2013; Astarita, 2018), where wage labour manufactured commodities, which would be sold on the market. The cost of labour and production would be less than the revenue from the sale, hence a profit would be generated (Marx, 2013). In Marxist terms, this is about the creation of 'surplus value' (Hill, 2013, p. 145). Although Marx and Engels (2015) claimed that it was the rise in trades and rapidly growing markets that resulted in the transition from feudalism to capitalism, as the previous manufacturing system was unable to meet the ever-increasing demands of the markets, it is important to note that ideas around the transition from feudalism to capitalism are highly contested. Some believe that

2   *The neoliberal capitalism and education*

capitalism first developed alongside feudalism, as feudal lords profited from capitalism while still holding power (Astarita, 2018). Others believe that capitalism developed in areas with little influence of feudal lords (Kriedte, Medick, and Schlumbohm, 1981), while yet others suggest that a 'partial' 'expropriation of some peasants' led to a number of individuals becoming landowners and working for feudal lords while others turned into 'marginalized vagabonds' that 'combined occasional work with crime' (Astarita, 2018, p. 253). Irrespective of the veracity of these theories of the history of the development of capitalism, a key point to highlight is that history is changeable, and this is an important lesson for creating optimism about transformation away from neoliberal capitalism.

Returning to the ideas of Marx, he notes that 'the dissolution of' feudalism 'set free the elements of' capitalism in the fourteenth and fifteenth centuries (Marx, 2013, p. 502). In *Capital*, Marx describes how English peasants became the proletariat by losing their land as well as their means of production when 'suddenly and forcibly torn from their means of subsidence, and hurled as free and "unattached" proletarians on the labour market' (Marx, 2013, p. 503). All these proletarians were left with was their labour power and so the individual became 'a free seller of labour power, who carries his commodity wherever he finds a market' (Marx, 2013, p. 503). Additionally, Astarita (2018, p. 254) illustrates the conditions that enabled a development towards capitalism and lists 'a relatively high circulation of money and merchandise as well as cash rents' and the 'sharp social differentiations' within villagers who owned significant acreage of land and those who did not that were forced to become wage labourers. With regard to the transition to the era of industrial capitalism, it is important to consider the increasing demand, not only for goods but also the need for further demand itself to expand and establish the system. Accordingly, capitalists have always sought ways to create further demands and concomitant markets in order to accumulate additional capital continuously; this has led to imperialism and empire-building, now reconfigured as globalisation. Marx and Engels (2015, p. 7) highlighted this point: 'the need of a constantly expanding market for products chases the bourgeoisie over the whole surface of the globe', driven 'by the conquest of new markets' and 'a more thorough exploitation of old ones'. As capitalism developed and established, so too did its capacity to eradicate barriers to its expansion through creating the political-economic and sociocultural as well as technological infrastructure to create greater potential for capital accumulation and surplus value.

In addition to the capitalists' insatiable appetite for surplus value as the driving force of capitalist development, class struggle is also implicated in developing capitalism. During the 1960s, after an unpublished chapter of

Marx's *Capital* emerged, a number of scholars from the Italian New Left began to reinterpret Marx's work on the accumulation of capital (Bowring, 2004). As a result, several scholars concluded, 'instead of the forces of production expanding according to their own autonomous logic, ... the accumulation of capital was ... driven by class struggle' (Bowring, 2004, p. 104). The fact that capitalists rely on wage labourers to create capital for surplus value means that they are at the behest of workers selling their capacity to labour; put another way, the capitalist system relies on workers and without them, the system breaks down. Therefore, it can be argued that it is the resistance, or at least the potential of resistance, of labourers that drives capitalists to be in ever search of development and expansion. Quite simply, capitalists are forced to create new ways (innovations) that sustain the subordination of the workers to keep them in line, and this is illustrated by creating the fear of being replaced by cheaper labour or automation. This is reflected in the argument by Cleaver (1992, p. 6) who notes 'technological change was often introduced in response to workers struggles' which 'could ... be seen as the introduction of new division of labour aimed at restoring control'. We return to this theme later in the books with regard to university work.

Returning to the accumulation of capital and the production of commodities, it has to be highlighted that Marx saw commodities as a crucial element of capitalist society (2013, p. 17). He describes commodities as an 'object outside us' – at a different level of reality, that is desired by someone (ibid.; Maisuria, 2017b) and therefore has exchange value. Marx also describes labour power as a commodity, which is different from material goods, which are a general class of commodities. As Rikowski (2017, p. 32) crucially highlights, according to Marx labour power 'exists within the body of the labourer' and is the only commodity 'that can create new value', making the labourer a necessary component of the production of commodities itself. So, uniquely the labour is a commodity itself and also labour power has the capacity to produce other commodities; no other commodity is like this.

The general class of commodities needs demand, and the capitalists create demand where it does not exist; thus, in order to accumulate further capital, a workforce is needed to meet these demands. This is where the education system becomes an important utility. Educational institutions in capitalism are necessitated to produce human capital, the labour power needed to be involved in the production of commodities. As Bowles and Gintis (1976) highlight, schooling creates and enhances the productivity of individuals by teaching skills that make them more employable as well as more motivated to be involved in capitalism, albeit without consciousness of doing so. While producing workers, the education system simultaneously facilitates young people's transition from education into the labour force, by mirroring and thus perpetuating the hierarchical structures they will encounter within their workplace, hence education serves a socialising function (ibid.). In the words of Hill (2004, p. 39; Hatcher, 2001), the aim of education is to 'produce compliant, ideologically indoctrinated, pro-capitalist, effective workers'.

As capitalism developed, so did its education system. From the nineteenth century, there has been an increasing stratification in types of educational establishments that reflect and (re)produce the class structure of society. This is evident in schooling with the emergence of fee-paying private schools out of public schools (the latter originated as open access schools for religious advancement [Maisuria, 2017a]). In contemporary capitalism, children who have been privately educated will most likely find themselves with opportunities for leading or managing occupational positions. This point was recognised by Gramsci (1971, p. 10) who stated that 'school is the instrument through which intellectuals of *various* levels are elaborated' (emphasis added). Furthermore, in capitalism, by being part of the state apparatus, schools are designed to 'work in the interest of the capital', which results in the education system being 'inherently hierarchical and elitist' (Hill, 2013, p. 148). Thus, education is a tool that produces large groups of people that will take up their subordinate workforce place within the production hierarchy (ibid.). Therein, "production" in schools is 'dominated by the imperatives of profit and domination rather than human need' (Bowles and Gintis, 1976, p. 54), which conditions the nature of education in capitalism.

Jaeger (2017) suggests that it makes economic sense for the capitalist system to designate successful as well as unsuccessful children and adults, the design is that the latter will be future 'workers who will accept low-level, part-time jobs without benefits' (pp. 975–977). She also highlights the economy's need for "middle class failures", who facilitate the façade of meritocracy (Maisuria, 2018) without "rocking the boat" (Jaeger, 2017, p. 976). Additionally, those from middle- and upper-class backgrounds, regardless of their abilities, particularly benefit from their own and their parents' social networks. These networks – their social capital – are described as 'connections which can be mobilized for particular purposes' and can be considered a 'distinctive resource' (Nash, 1990, p. 432). Therefore, these networks and social ties are a resource that the middle and upper class can exploit in the labour market and increasingly so in education (Maisuria, 2017a). In this context, it becomes easy to blame wealthier parents and those parents who game the system, for choosing certain schools or for utilising their social connections in order to improve their children's chances in life. However, Wrigley (2012) highlights how this overlooks capitalism's role in creating inequity, and it does not lead anywhere – what

Green and Kynaston (2019) term 'the dead-end politics of hypocrisy'. The bigger picture, Wrigley contends, is that the strategies of wealthier parents in school selection should be seen as a self-preservation response to the fact that the stakes are so high. Individualism and self-interest are a foundational component of capitalism; ethical solidarity, collegiality, and comradeship is purposefully difficult. The finger of blame should be pointed at the system rather than the individual because the system has been designed as a zero-sum game, where one's successes are the result of others' failures (Giroux, 2016). This is the cut-throat nature of capitalism and the way that it plays out in education.

While capitalism has been the dominant hegemony, its dominance is not hermetically sealed as an inevitability. The potential to overcome capitalism is highlighted by many 'resistance theorists' and critical revolutionary pedagogues who emphasise 'possibilities for teachers and students challenging' the current system and engage 'in liberatory and transformative education' (Hill, 2013, p. 146). Paraphrasing Hill (2013), McLaren et al. (2004, p. 138) state that a teacher should be a 'transformative intellectual who does not instruct students what to think but who learns to think dialectically and who develops a critical consciousness aimed at social transformation'. Therefore, teachers are in a unique position where they equip students with skills, competences, abilities, knowledge, and the attitudes and personal qualities that can be expressed and expended in the capitalist labour process (Hill and Kumar, 2009, p. 20), and they can concurrently influence their students to think critically about the social structure and possibilities of change. In this way, raising criticality and class consciousness is a fundamental role for the effective teacher (Maisuria, 2017b). Thus, teachers are potentially 'dangerous' to capitalism, as they can undo the efforts of an education system and social structure that aim to train individuals to be 'compliant, ideologically indoctrinated, pro-capitalist, effective workers' (Hill, 2004, p. 39; Giroux, 2016). In this context, it is logical that capitalism circumscribes the autonomy and freedom of educators by, inter alia, an audit culture and surveillance. These are issues that we return to.

On the issues of ideology and culture, it is important to highlight that while a substantial increase of wealth and subsequently the improvement of living standards in general have been attributed to the economic system of capitalism, the capitalist system has an inability to distribute wealth fairly, creating mass economic inequality and social problems (see for example More, 2002; Lippit, 2005; Fisher, 2009). Earlier, we subjected the individualism and self-interest fundamental in capitalism to negative critique in the context of school choice; according to adherents of Margaret Thatcher's politics, these are claimed as beneficial for the economy and therefore also for the whole population as it allegedly would 'lift all boats' (Lippit, 2005, p. 2). However, it is clear that this proposition has not materialised given historic level of inequality within nations, regions, and globally. Markets, private ownership, and individuals' and businesses' pursuit of capital and profit have been prioritised and increasingly so, while egalitarian values and the welfare of the majority in society exist in political rhetoric only, for the most part (Giroux, 2014).

In *The Communist Manifesto* and the volumes of *Capital*, Marx and Engels highlight the detrimental impacts of capitalism for the majority of people, nevertheless they acknowledge its economic necessity for socialism. They were clear that capitalism was a necessary stage for the eventual development of socialism. This necessity was due to the capacity of capitalism to create rapid and exponential economic and technological development, which would be needed by socialism for people to flourish through redistribution. Also, they suggested a sociocultural development through capitalism too, specifically that the globalising of the capitalist system would enable nations to share properties, material as well as intellectual, leveraging nations away from 'national one-sidedness and narrow-mindedness' and allowing access to world literature (Marx, 2013, p. 7).

The essence of Marx and Engels's work was on capital, and in the development of this scholarship was also the importance of social class, which would define capitalist society. It is necessary to identify the antagonistic relationship between the two classes in society, the 'vast majority (workers)' and the 'small minority (owners and managers)' who control them (Bowles and Gintis, 1976, p. 54). Described by Marx as the proletariat and the bourgeoisie respectively, their relationship is distinguished by the bourgeoisie's need (or rather quest) for capital accumulation and surplus value. Therefore, the proletariat, employed by the bourgeoisie, 'are the primary producers of wealth due to the expenditure of their labor in the production of commodities' in a capitalist society (Hill, 2013, p. 145). This wealth largely, however, continues to stay in the hands of the bourgeoisie as they own the means of production and therefore consequently own the accumulated wealth. In the continuous quest for more wealth, the bourgeoisie's focus on 'extracting from labor as much work as possible in return for the lowest possible wages' (Bowles and Gintis, 1976, p. 54) forces the labourer to work harder for less. Not only are these labourers paid less than their work is worth, Bowles and Gintis (1976, p. 57) stress the 'absence of alternative sources of livelihood', which subsequently leaves individuals no choice but to comply with increasing demands (Rikowski, 2017). Today, as a result, 'millions of workers are being exploited by a relatively small yet strategically powerful global ruling class driven by an unshakable desire for accumulation of profit' (McLaren and Farahmandpur, 2001, p. 137). In this situation, the proletariat's situation has become even more precarious due to the development of 'techniques of production' that 'reduce the amount of living labour' in order to keep remuneration costs low (Livingstone and Scholtz, 2016, p. 472), a point that will be discussed in more detail shortly, and specified to education.

We have stressed the capitalists' need to keep costs low while at the same time accumulating more and more wealth through the creation of demands and expansion of markets, and with this understanding the process of globalisation is important. As highlighted by Olssen and Peters (2005), globalisation was largely enabled by technological advancement that allowed nations to communicate and share ideas, allowing them to transcend previous borders and boundaries. Importantly globalisation also facilitated the rise of a new phase in capitalism – neoliberalism.

Neoliberal turn

Although not given the name of neoliberalism yet, it was aggressively advanced after the election of Margaret Thatcher in UK and Ronald Reagan in the US, who claimed that Keynesianism was to blame for weak economic growth and a reliance on welfare (see Harvey, 2007; Fitzner, 2017). Neoliberalism was a long time in development. In 1947, at its first official meeting, the Mont Pèlerin Society, consisting of a number of intellectuals and economists, identified a 'lack of alternatives to the existing (Keynesian) order' (Srnicek and Williams, 2015, p. 55). As a result, the neoliberal doctrine, a reformed version of liberalism, was created to establish unfettered and expanded markets to harness individual choice. However, at this point in history, Keynesianism as the dominant political hegemony was deeply rooted and garnered commitment, and the neoliberal project would need to be strategically implemented as a long-term political project (Srnicek and Williams, 2015). Eventually, the economic recession of the 1970s was an opportunity for the neoliberals to attribute political failure to Keynesianism. A report disseminated amongst the neoliberal reformers in the 1970s highlighted the need to bring 'value-oriented intellectuals' of left-wing persuasion and 'journalists who favour "the cause of humanity"' under control (Sklar, 1980, p. 40). Especially, progressive educators and those working within the media were seen as a threat to certain individuals working within the 'world of high finance', and thus needed to be made more 'governable and more able to service capital' (Davies and Bansel, 2007, p. 250). Neoliberal policies introduced in education from the 1980s began the attempted wholesale destruction of educators with left-wing, progressive, and liberal commitments, and education systems based on these values (Giroux, 2014; Maisuria, 2015).

The UK economic recession of the 1970s had challenged the commitment to an expensive welfare society, and with the rate of unemployment increasing (Allen and Ainley, 2007), neoliberalism became a politically feasible

8 *The neoliberal capitalism and education*

and supposedly necessary solution. While the rise in unemployment could plausibly be attributed to the economic recession, teachers were widely being blamed for not adequately preparing young people for the labour workforce. Consequently, an increased focus on 'the schools' role in preparing the future generation to contribute to the country's economic success was articulated' at the time (Wyse and Torrance, 2009, p. 214) and paved the way for the neoliberal principles that would have a tremendous impact on education. Looking for solutions to improve economic problems faced by the nation, the ruling capitalist class seemed to have found those in the work of the Mont Pèlerin Society (Srnicek and Williams, 2015). According to Peck and Tickell (2002), the process of neoliberalisation consists of three phases, described as "proto" neoliberalism, "roll-back" neoliberalism, and "roll-out" neoliberalism. The first stage, "proto", is described as an 'intellectual project', established by 'economic and libertarian theorists' in order to offer an alternative to the 'political and economic crisis around the Keynesian welfare state' (Ball, 2012, p. 3). At this point, the Mont Pèlerin Society provided the 'invisible framework of political common sense that was formed by the ideas circulating in elite networks' they had established (Srnicek and Williams, 2015, p. 55). The second stage, the "roll-back", is then characterised by an 'active destruction and discreditation of Keynesian-welfarist and social-collectivist institutions' (Peck and Tickell, 2002, p. 384). Marked as inefficient, social services and public goods such as education are then taken apart and (quasi-) privatised in the last stage, the "roll-out".

The Mont Pèlerin Society had found support of their philosophical and political-economic project in Thatcher and Reagan, and neoliberalism became central to every governing decision of the ruling capitalist class, including globally through international structures such as the World Bank and World Trade Organisation and distinct trading blocs, such as the European Union. This was a defining moment in history. Subsequently, higher education was also gradually being restructured too, which would eventually lead to a 'subordination of academic governance, professional identities, and intellectual cultures to market rationalities' (Amsler, 2011, p. 63) with marketisation, privatisation, and commodification as the three 'dimensions of education becoming capitalised' (Rikowski, 2017, p. 43).

Higher education for creating labour and productivity

Similar to the 1970s in the UK, circa 2008 the core capitalist nations experienced an economic crisis that was characterised by slow or no economic growth, high levels of unemployment and underemployment, and low levels of investment (Bellamy Foster and Yates, 2014; Hall, 2015a). While as described earlier, capitalism is responsible for an increase in general wealth within capitalist nations, many academics and commentators, such as Danny Dorling and Oxfam, highlight the astronomical disparity in wealth and income within capitalist nations and the vast inequality this entails. One of the key indices of inequality is income distribution. Instead of acknowledging inequality and economic crises as a sign of failure of the capitalist system, individuals' unemployment or low income is blamed on their level of productivity, their willingness to work and to invest in their human capital (Bellamy Foster and Yates, 2014, p. 4). The idea of investing in education to increase the value of one's human capital is not only beneficial to the individual, but also to the neoliberal capitalism. This benefit derives from the fact that there is a global competition for innovation and enterprise that improves economic productivity. Moreover, neoliberalism further benefits from human capital theory because if there are more workers with increasingly stronger credentials, then there is increased competition for jobs, and employment positions are more likely to be precarious by virtue of the fact that there are increasingly qualified replacements available, which could drive down pay and worsen conditions. As Allen (2019) highlights, according to the Office for National Statistics, one in six adults in the UK are overqualified for the job they do. Not only does this raise the standard for new applicants, it also means that gaining more credentials becomes a necessity (ibid.), driving ever more people into university education and the financial debt this incurs, which is itself useful for capitalist banks and loans companies because the debt is for life for most students the horrors of this are noted in the foreword by Peter McLaren. This flags the exploitations inherent in neoliberalism. The human capital interest for neoliberalism means a burgeoning marketplace has been created in higher education with demand corresponding to institutional prestige and potential job opportunities for students after graduating. The student has been reconstructed and is now a consumer; in this environment, the university degree is now a commodity.

As Maisuria and Cole (2017) argue, the consumerist attitude created in students, especially due to the White Paper entitled *Putting Students at the Heart of Higher Education* published in 2011 but initiated during the Blair years, has created a classroom ethos that a degree award is the result of an exchange of money, not ideas, and anything less than a 2:1 grade or a first is not 'value for money' and a poor 'investment' (phrases that appear consistently in the 2015 Green Paper and subsequent Education Bill), rendering it in essence a commodity with varying interest. Students in English universities are no longer reading for a degree, they are encouraged to perceive themselves as buying a degree, and this is now enshrined in law. Students in English universities are (financially) protected by the Competition and Markets Authority (CMA), which lays out *consumer* rights in relation to purchasing a degree, rendering a university learning experience and qualification no different to choosing from which supermarket to buy a product. With these consumer rights comes the possibility of students filing litigation charges against universities (it is unclear how individual lecturers are implicated in such cases). With this policy agenda increasingly commodifying the university learning experience and qualification, universities are becoming concerned with consumer law to the extent that they are training academics in their legal duty as part of the consumer contract. The policy agenda is radically deepening the neoliberalisation of the once-public university and the nature of the learning and teaching experience.

As part of commodification comes a demand-side economics and the university becomes part of the marketised landscape. Within this marketised landscape however, the 'scarce resources' of the 'deregulated education market' (Amsler, 2011, p. 63) put new restraints on universities. For these universities, student fees have become a necessary source of income, as they enable the university to function with reduced government funding. This is consistent with the neoliberal idea that the State should be minimal and even abolished, only existing as 'a skeleton regulatory and monitoring agency' (Dexter, 2001, in Allen and Ainley, 2007, p. 82). The significantly reduced government funding that is available however, has to be "earned" by universities competing with one another in form of performativity, outcome measures, and statistics (ibid.); earned (instead of public service) is another concept very much in alignment with the capitalist and neoliberal mindset that emphasises competition within the market. These issues, pertaining to performativity, competition, and student fees, will be explored in more detail in the second chapter.

Universities have been increasingly scrutinised for not producing graduates equipped to become a part of the labour workforce (Zajda and Rust, 2016). As explained earlier, for the capitalist system, human capital plays a central role to create increasing capacity in the form of labour power to produce commodities (Marx, 2013). While Becker (1964, p. 17) suggests that 'the earnings of more educated people are almost always well above average', seeing individuals in terms of human capital and education as an investment purely for individual financial gain has been increasingly criticised. Human capital theory is described as problematic for various reasons. While it ignores the holistic value and worth of education beyond employment, i.e. social, emotional, cultural development, it also prioritises making the nation attractive for industries and employers looking to invest in an environment with low-cost well-qualified workers (Giroux, 2014, p. 180; Zajda, 2018, p. 5). Additionally and most importantly, human capital theory suggests a 'linear continuum' between 'education, work, productivity and earnings' and assumes that 'higher education more or less automatically triggers private enrichment, career success and national economic growth' (Marginson, 2019, p. 1). While it cannot be denied that at some point an investment in the expansion of higher education with the 'goal of equality of opportunity' enabled some capacity for upward social mobility while being beneficial for the economy (ibid., p. 2), the current context is more complicated and the idea of the 'knowledge economy' can be used as an example for the failure of human capital theory.

Knowledge economy

The term "knowledge economy", first introduced in the 1960s, 'derives from the idea that knowledge and education can be treated as a business product', while 'educational and innovative intellectual products and services ... can be exported for a high-value return' (Ball, 2017, p. 25). In a knowledge economy, the emphasis is on producing knowledge, ideas, and information (ibid.), rather than manufactured goods, which had been the country's assets especially after World War II. It was believed that 'knowledge and its application' would replace 'labour as the source of "added value"' (Bell, 1973, p. 506) as manufacturing goods were commonly being produced at much lower cost in countries such as India or China. The new way of generating employment was 'through enterprising activities' rather than by simply 'skilling the young and reskilling the old', as enterprising activities would favour competition in the global market (Ainley and Allen, 2010, p. 29). Additionally, technological advancement and the associated sharing of new innovations that replace old ideas at rapid speed had led to companies and nations more generally being in a constant race to stay relevant to optimise productivity (Ball, 2017). Accordingly, investing in the knowledge economy and thus creating a workforce with high-level skills were considered to lead to the innovation that Britain needed to compete in the global market, while simultaneously creating new jobs (Lauder et al., 2012). Consequently, the assumption that 'knowledge has become the central "factor of production" in an advanced, developed economy' has been widely adopted since the 1960s (Drucker, 1969, p. 248).

In order to advance a knowledge economy, the government turned to education, especially higher education institutions, for the production of "knowledge workers" (human capital) that were "desperately needed" for a more productive economy. In order to facilitate this shift, access to higher education was widened by removing the cap on the number of students who could be admitted, and student numbers increased (Ainley and Allen, 2010). It is noteworthy that this shift for universities was accompanied by a whole new language, which is normally associated with profit-making private sector business, and in addition universities were moved to the *Business* Department of Governmental Affairs [our emphasis]. This is all reflected in a Department for Business Innovation and Skills' publication (2009, p. 7) asserting that 'in a knowledge economy, universities are the most important mechanism we have for generating ... and transforming knowledge'. It does not only distinguish the role universities play in establishing a knowledge economy, but it also "sells" the idea of attending university to the public. This is echoed in the 2016 White Paper (Department for Business Innovation and Skills, 2016), which maintains that 'higher education continues to be a sound financial and personal investment with a wide range of social benefits' (p. 7) and that 'graduates are central' to the country's 'prosperity and success as a knowledge economy' (p. 8). As 'education is increasingly viewed primarily in terms of its productive capacity' (Ball, 2017, p. 27), several problems emerge that impact considerably on the nature of higher education.

Firstly, promoted as a way to tackle the country's unemployment, educating people to become part of the highly skilled workforce required by the knowledge economy did not have the desired impacts. This is partly because the expected developments that would have required a large number of "knowledge workers", if they existed, were interrupted by 'the financial crisis of 2008 and the subsequent economic recession' (Lauder et al., 2012, p. 1). The recession resulted in a surge in unemployment as businesses were unable or reluctant to hire new people, had to employ those who required less pay, or simply had to let people go (Ainley and Allen, 2010). Additionally, it has been pointed out that those jobs, which according to the government needed filling, do not exist. Ball (2017, p. 30), for example, illustrates that little has changed within the domestic economy and that 'the proportion of economic activity involving new technologies and "new science" ... remains relatively modest', while the service sector remains by far the strongest sector to account for the nation's employment. Therefore, the much-demanded innovative knowledge worker does not seem to be needed as much after all.

Having many unemployed graduates desperately looking for jobs crystallises the exploitation that is part of neoliberalism. Marx describes the industrial reserve army or surplus-population, referring to a large group of people, who are 'always ready for exploitation', at the capitalist's behest (Marx, 2013, p. 440). Not only can they be employed at an instant to 'increase the activity of their operations when required' (ibid., p. 442), but they also function as a way of disciplining existing workers. Should a labourer be unhappy with his or her working conditions, a replacement would be readily available and would thus allow the employer to dispose of the existing employee, without having to fear a decrease in productivity.

Additionally, the capitalist can use this surplus worker population as a way to drive down labour cost when he or she replaces skilled workers with less skilled workers and is thus able to buy more labour power with the same capital (ibid.). Accordingly, those educated for the non-existent jobs within the knowledge economy have themselves become a reserve army. Their unemployment leaves them desperate enough to work for little pay; they accept jobs for which they are overqualified; and employers have a never-ending pool of potential workers to choose from, which makes it easy for them to "hire and fire" whenever it suits them. The reserve army, which is called casualised work in academic industrial relations terms, is a major issue for trade unions today. The power of Trade Unions in England were substantively destroyed by Thatcher and later by David Cameron precisely to enable employers to gain the upper-hand by lessening the capacity of workers to collectively resist exploitative working conditions and poor pay.

The second concern about a knowledge economy is about 'reinforcing systematic social inequalities and exacerbating economic and social polarization' (Ball, 2017, p. 30). In order to partake in the knowledge economy, technological advancements (e.g. high speed Internet) and skills to use them are crucial; however, parts of the nation do not have access to it or cannot use it, which essentially excludes them and thus leads to a divide between those "wired" and those "unwired" (ibid.). This concern relates to what we have discussed earlier with regard to claims about capitalism, where its purported benefits do not benefit everyone in the nation to the same extent and it actually exacerbates inequalities instead. Where individuals are blamed for not seeing educational qualifications as a way to further their careers and to become more "employable" (Ainley and Allen, 2010), others' success and the associated paycheck are attributed to their ability to recognise the opportunity as well as to select the right university (Marginson, 2019). This is another example of economics trumping egalitarianism and ethics.

While these issues are important, the third issue is most relevant for our argument in this book. It relates to the commodification of education and knowledge. Through increasingly neoliberal education policies, education has been subject to commodification for close to four decades. Striving for a knowledge economy intensifies this neoliberalisation and results in knowledge itself becoming a commodity by virtue of the introduction of tuition fees and also the language of "investment" being peddled by successive governments. Additionally, those people who were once considered part of the knowledge economy's highly skilled workforce, in 'professional and managerial occupations' [,] are now 'experiencing degradation of their working conditions, increasing unemployment' (Livingstone and Scholtz, 2016, p. 472), regardless of their "investment in education" which was promised to "pay off".

This is also true for other professions, such as teachers and further education lecturers. Educators, who are crucial in the production of the future labour force now face similar struggles to the young people they "produce", and those working in academia are coerced to sell their labour below what it ought to be worth. Additionally, they have to be willing to engage in neoliberalising the university nature and function, such as through marketing campaigns and mendacious claims, for example, about employability. At the same time, as 'maintaining the ideological conditions of the reproduction of capitalist social relations' (Malott and Ford, 2015, p. 107), educators have been faced with increasingly precarious working conditions and uncertain futures. Life as an academic in the neoliberal university has become a grim reality for many as we shall report.

2 Neoliberalisation of the university and academic work

Competition and (Quasi-)privatisation

The 2008 economic crisis faced by capitalist nations has deepened the neoliberalisation of the nature and structure of higher education. In England, the main country of our focus, there has been a financialisation of higher education that has intensified and reconfigured universities in a competitively corporate manner, making them run like businesses (c.f. Canaan and Shumar, 2008, p. 3; Beckmann, Cooper, and Hill, 2009). Put another way, the front and centring of the finances aspect of universities has changed their very nature, with a concomitant prioritisation of marketing the university as a product to attract customers and to build the university as a brand for consumption.

This shift has resulted in an appetite for datafication, this is the gathering and monitoring of metrics for comparison, which is published for advertising and league table compilation. This data plays a key role in marketisation, as it offers the opportunity for universities to produce comparable data sets that can "confirm" their quality. In this environment, all elements of the university life are available as measures for gaining a competitive edge. Teaching and learning are considered a tradable commodity with exchange value, but for it to be sold, the university must show quality through metrics relating to levels of 'excellence' (Maisuria and Cole, 2017); this quite simply boils down to employability in an age of human capital prioritisation. This neoliberal scenario changes the nature of the university, and also the role, function, and purpose of academic labour.

The refocusing of university work to focus primarily on narrowly defined skills acquisition, competencies, and training aligns with predictions made in *The Communist Manifesto* through proletarianisation that emerges in capitalism. Marx and Engels (2015, p. 13) suggest that 'the lower strata of the middle class – the small tradespeople, shopkeepers, ... handicraftsmen and peasants' would eventually 'sink gradually into the proletariat', as 'their specialized skill is rendered worthless' in changed conditions of existence where capitalism is more developed, a statement that seems to apply to many, if not most, who work within academia. In Marxist terms, "proletarianisation" essentially describes the movement into the proletariat, the downward movement from a higher social status in the working class to a lower one. Gill and Pratt (2008, p. 2) point out that while historically lower-skilled and lower-paid workers in the capitalist system have always been subjected to precarious working conditions and were engaged in irregular and insecure labour, even those who were previously considered high-status workers, such as academics, have now joined 'this group of "precarious workers"'. Accordingly, the following section will examine the factors that have led to this development, for example, the role of technology, the alienation of labourers from their work, the increase of competition between and within institutions and the "performance culture". As a point of departure, it is important to recognise that performativity is not designed to be a function that enhances the public service nature of education, but rather a feature of privatisation.

There has not yet been a mass privatisation of universities in England. In other words, they still function as non-profit-making organisations partially funded by taxpayers' money, but many aspects have been outsourced and they operate largely to bolster neoliberalism and promote individualism – hence we say quasi-privatised. This has been a trend in all public institutions since the 1980s, and it has deepened and extended 'the rule of capital' (Rikowski, 2017, p. 30). Significant cutbacks in government funding increasingly force universities to generate their own income and commodify their operations, essentially turning them into businesslike corporations (Giroux, 2003). Many institutions form partnerships with (sometimes rather dubious) for-profit businesses, such as the arms industry or the military in order to gain resources (Doward and Bennett, 2018; Webb, 2018; Zhou, 2017), and competition with other institutions is now considered inevitable and natural for survival. The cut-throat competitiveness seen in the private sector has become normalised for universities, exactly as those pushing the neoliberal agenda had intended.

One way for universities to generate State income is to participate in research. 'Research achievements and reputations as reflected in citations, grants and awards' are necessary for the university to demonstrate its relevance and supposed excellence (Leathwood and Read, 2013, p. 1162; Maisuria and Cole, 2017). For this reason, 'the research activities and outputs of individuals, departments and institutions' are constantly monitored and evaluated (Leathwood and Read, 2013, p. 1163). This, according to Webb (2018, p. 96), discourages 'long-term research while encouraging research fraud' instead. Fraud is a provocative term, but ethics are at stake when academics, often through coercion to satisfy performativity, 'apply for grants in which' they 'have no academic interest but will look good on departmental returns or income' or submit 'unfinished or unoriginal' journal articles 'in order to chalk up another "count" in the annual "output" review' (Ball, 2000, p. 8). Especially when the Research Excellence Framework that measures the performance of academics is looming, Smith (2000, p. 33) notes the desperation that journal editors (who are also academics) are confronted with when authors 'want to know if their paper can be turned around in a few weeks and be published a couple of months later' even when rejected previously. In addition to this, Porschitz, Smircich, and Calás (2016, p. 246) highlight how private corporations that have entered partnerships with universities especially benefit 'from university research and teaching' while it is the students who are 'carrying the costs (not always equally) for university activities that may not directly serve their own personal interests'. The whole research-funding industry is set up to reproduce the prestige and power of universities with a strong research identity. Non-research-intensive universities cannot compete because money follows research outputs, building more capacity to engage in future research. This widening stratification is exemplified by the Research England's statistics on research grants: in 2018/2019, the University of East London, a widening participation university with a strong civic focus received £3 million, while University of Oxford received £149 million (Research England, 2018). In neoliberalism, public service is not valued and rewarded. With reduced State funding, universities with a civic ethos will increasingly struggle. In this environment, academics who have an interest and skills in research and scholarship are being forced to gravitate towards research-intensive universities, while newer and prospective academics will be forced to concentrate on teaching, with large classes and a curriculum focusing on skills, competencies, and training for employment.

Nationally, using the data collected through performance management and monitoring, universities are ranked in league tables that are used to compare universities and their "success" with respect to specific markers of quality. While US universities have been ranked since the late nineteenth century, university rankings in the UK only emerged in the 1990s, where they were part of the neoliberal restructuring of education with increased competition, an audit culture, and institutional discipline (Amsler and Bolsmann, 2012). These league table rankings are not only used by prospective students but also by government agencies to constantly monitor and compare the "performance" of universities in relation to national agendas, the current one being a preoccupation with productivity as part of a national industrial strategy. Additionally, rankings support the agenda to turn 'institutions of the public good into corporations and brands'

(Amsler and Bolsmann, 2012, p. 284), by functioning as a tool that helps "selling the product" to consumers – again it is worthwhile reflecting on the shift in language. While functioning as an advertisement for prospective students, the league table position of a university also distinguishes whether funding opportunities, for instance, doctoral grants, will be available for a particular institution. This is problematic for several reasons.

Firstly, government funding is frequently 'directed towards research that serves private corporate interests' (Washburn, 2015, referenced in Porschitz, Smircich, and Calás, 2016, p. 345), as well as towards 'disciplines that can evidence contribution to economic growth' (Maisuria, 2011, p. 288). The problem with this is that higher education and its research focuses become in the servitude of private interest, rather than the common good. It also means that so-called blue-skies thinking, that encourages freedom to spur imaginative ideas, becomes circumscribed. Secondly, above we have highlighted that universities' performance differs greatly depending on their resources, with those having a lot regularly outperforming those with little (Lynch and Baines, 2004). Considering research grants given by the government, it is worth pointing out that last year the University of Oxford announced taking part in various research projects that are funded by the government 'to boost research commercialization' (University of Oxford, 2018a). While it is stated that the projects are funded by Research England, a '£100m fund that supports university collaboration in research commercialization' to share 'good practice across the higher education sector', it also states 'helping deliver the government's industrial strategy priorities' as one of its aims, clearly showing that neoliberalism and education are in cahoots (ibid.). Additionally, it is worth noting that the other universities involved in these collaborative projects are the University of Sheffield, London School of Economics and Political Science (LSE), Cambridge University, University of Manchester, University of Sussex, and Newcastle University, almost all of which, except the University of Sussex, are "coincidentally" Russell Group universities, who are, as described by the University of Exeter's website, 'universities committed to maintaining the very best research, an outstanding teaching and learning experience and unrivalled links with business and the public sector' (University of Exeter, no date). Thus, the project that "boosts commercialisation" does not only prioritise financial gain generally, but it also predominantly involves universities that are already better off than others. Additionally, there seems to be a strong relationship between the location of universities and their funding opportunities. Adams (2017) highlights, for example, that a quarter of all government funding in the UK goes to the "golden triangle", consisting of the universities of Oxford, Cambridge, and a number of London-based universities, and that they, along with

52 other universities in the south-east receive more than half of all government funding, while 77 universities in the 'midlands, Yorkshire, the north and the west' have to share the remaining 48 percent. This is indicative of unfairness and stratification in a variety of ways.

These conditions clearly highlight that some universities are at a structural and political disadvantage compared to others and as noted above, that this disadvantage subsequently impacts on their opportunities to generate future funding, as funding is largely given to those who are already producing results for neoliberal interests and can thus be considered as performing well. Additionally, it has been pointed out that where funding is available, it is 'primarily directed towards some elite departments classified as internationally excellent' (Lynch and Baines, 2004, p. 176) but academic programmes in the arts, social sciences, and humanities that are not easily linked to economic productivity are marginalised and therefore receive little to no funding, leaving their finances to come from student fees. This, however, is rarely sufficient and in the future these programmes will probably shrink, close down, or become commercialised for private sector funding. All of this indicates a subject/discipline hierarchy through which neoliberal control is administered. Amsler and Bolsmann (2012, p. 284) elaborate and argue that the whole ranking system is part of the 'politico-ideological technologies of valuation and hierarchisation that operate according to a principle logic of inclusion and exclusion', instead of being 'neutral methods for understanding the quality or value of education'. Thus, while they are considered to be an indicator of the quality of an institution, league tables simply perpetuate the idea that some institutions are superior as they are 'heavily mediated by marketing rhetoric' (ibid. p. 285), while deprioritising other factors that, from the perspective of educators, would be a better sign of quality, such as contribution to society building.

Student fees have become a crucial source of income for institutions to off-set the enormous cuts that previously socialised goods, such as education and healthcare, have been subjected to (Davies, 2014). Since introduced in 1997/1998, tuition fees for university have increased ninefold (Bolton, 2017). Consequently, those studying in higher education institutions and thus paying for their degree are seen as consumers who *need* to be recruited by the university in order to generate enough income to sustain the institution. Under the guise of increasing the access to university, the cap to limit student numbers has been lifted (Osborne, 2013), allowing universities to accept as many students as they can possibly accommodate (and sometimes more!) in order to generate as much income as possible. The subsequent increase in student numbers shows the effectiveness of the human capital idea that a university education is an investment that will assure their future employment.

The need to recruit as many students as possible has led to a questionable culture, where academics are being coerced to play a recruiting role and getting "bums-on-seats" at any expense with all marketing potential fully exploited. Furedi (2009, p. 35) suggests that university 'courses are modified and made customer friendly' and academics construct the appearance that 'the expectations of students [customer] takes priority over intellectually challenging them'. Student recruitment is liable to fluctuate, and some universities have financially struggled as their student numbers decline, which has led to brand image reconsiderations, often using expensive consultants (while cutting staff and resource spending). While in the past, struggling universities were able to request assistance from the government to mitigate such difficulties, and managed to survive (Hillman, 2018), the new regulator responsible for universities, the Office for Students (OfS) with its conceptualisation of students as customers and a subsequent emphasis on value-for-money in terms of investment for future jobs, takes a laissez-faire approach preferring to not intervene when universities struggle (Evans, 2018; Fazackerley, 2018). In his speech, Sam Gyimah, short-lived as Minister for Education at the Department for *Business*, Energy and Industrial Strategy [our emphasis], stated that he is 'not just a university minister, but also a minister for students – placing a laser-like focus on students', while also demanding universities to provide 'excellent teaching, support and value for money' and to take 'advantages of the freedoms of the new regulatory system to offer new courses and modes of study to meet student needs' (Department for Education and Gyimah, 2018). Firstly, it must be noted that the name of the department represents exactly what the government prioritises. Secondly, his statement clearly shows his own priority in making sure that the students are satisfied customers of what universities have to offer. As Evans (2018) points out, in the eyes of the OfS, failing universities are not necessarily considered a problem as 'in a competition for survival, the strong win, while the weak fail'. In these conditions, many academics are traduced to being like a pawn of the university's manoeuvrings to maximise their potential to survive.

Within their recruitment offensive, league tables are necessary for universities to market how their institution as well as their individual departments 'are superior to their rivals' (Lynch and Baines, 2004, p. 177). There is a multiplicity of metrics used by universities, including expected future salary indices. Research by the Institute for Fiscal Studies (IFS) focusing on the salaries of graduates at UK universities shows 'significant variation in graduate earnings between universities', indicating significant stratification and inequality reproduction that is aligned with the social class background of their student profile. For example, graduates from LSE (a university with mainly middle/upper class students) earn 'around 70% more than the average graduate 5 years after graduation'

(Institute for Fiscal Studies, 2018, pp. 45–46). These differences are not only within institutions but also within areas of the country as the range in median salaries for graduates varies within regions. While in 2017, 21–30-year-old graduates in the East Midlands, West Midlands, and in the North East report the lowest salary of £22,000, graduates of the same age in London report a salary of £29,500 (Department for Education, 2018). As mentioned previously, government funding given to universities varies greatly between the South East/London and the other parts of the UK; thus, it might explain why graduates in those areas, who have potentially studied at these better-funded universities, can command a higher salary. The IFS data suggests that the high-status universities, meaning the Russell Group of universities, dominate the top of the earnings distribution hierarchy, while those established after 1992 and those categorised as "Other" 'predominantly make up the bottom half of institutions' (Institute for Fiscal Studies, 2018, p. 46). Oxford and Cambridge have the highest graduate salary outcomes, followed by London universities such as LSE and Imperial College, who are part of the "golden triangle". While these results are course-specific at the individual institutions and statistics suggest that in certain cases some smaller, less prestigious universities are exceptions, overall the salary of graduates from Russell Group universities are higher than that of others, even when differences in student demographics have been accounted for (Institute for Fiscal Studies, 2018). Thus, it is not surprising that elite universities use this data as part of their promotion activities. While the University of Oxford supplies statistics on salary distribution of graduates on their website (University of Oxford, 2018b), LSE highlights the IFS report stating that 'the Department of Education places History at LSE top of the table with earnings superior to any other university in the UK' (London School of Economics and Political Science, 2018). Therefore, graduate earning potential is emphasised by universities whose status and performance allow them to highlight their "success", further increasing their advantage compared to less prestigious universities. This all aligns with the idea that some universities, who can, essentially sell themselves as akin to luxury brands (Maisuria, 2011). The collateral damage in this zero-sum scenario comes by way of the negative impact on other universities and also their students, and of course their academics. As league tables and a focus on graduate salaries determine the value of students' degrees, it gives the appearance that some are more valuable than others (Canaan and Shumar, 2008), leaving those who are not affiliated to an elite institute to feel less worthy, and also be perceived in this way more widely.

In this marketised educational landscape, it is not surprising that the relationship between the academic and the student has changed. With the student paying fees to receive an education, their relationship is characterised by the student paying for a commodity supplied by the academic. Accordingly, the lecturer has to provide what the consumer or customer demands (Beckmann, Cooper, and Hill, 2009); therefore, the nature of the relationship is largely constructed by the students. While previously the "power" to lead and guide was in the hands of the lecturer, in this new arrangement the student as consumer gains power by paying for a commodity. There is thus a risk that he or she is potentially un/satisfied with the "quality", leaving the lecturer in a vulnerable position. With so much focus on generating income through recruitment, it can be questioned whether the university can in reality prioritise the students' needs and perceive them as more than an essential funding stream. For the academic, the neoliberal university has become something akin to a "sausage factory". This is a term that Rikowski (2012) borrows from Marx's (2013, p. 355) metaphor where he compares the 'teaching factory' (school) to a 'sausage factory'. Given the vulnerability and precarity of the academic in this scenario, the concept of the reserve army just waiting for an opportunity to be "of use" should not be forgotten.

Customer perception of quality in the form of student satisfaction metrics has become an integral part of the higher education system. Consequently, the National Student Survey (NSS), implemented in 2005, has become a mandatory survey for all universities in England, Wales, and Northern Ireland, where 'final-year undergraduates report their levels of "satisfaction" with their degree course' (Cruickshank, 2016, p. 8). More recently and in addition to other forms of measuring performance, "teaching excellence" has been put on the datafication agenda through the introduction of the Teaching Excellence Framework (TEF), thus to mirror the Research Excellence Framework (REF) and compliment the NSS. The idea of what constitutes excellence and how to measure this in quantifiable terms, or whether it can be done so, are highly contentious questions; however, "teaching excellence" has been made one of the priorities of the government and thus also for universities. Kallio, Kallio and Grossi (2017, p. 299) have described the general shift as the 'quantification game', where 'the easiest way of meeting targets is by lowering quality – for instance, by letting students pass exams more easily and granting degrees with looser criteria', or indeed, by simply teaching in a way that pleases the student consumers (see Maisuria and Cole, 2017). So expansive is the quantification game, that 'Students are forever being asked what they think about the teaching they receive'; surveys assess not only their satisfaction but also their engagement and they are provided with tools to rate and rank academics internally by the university and also externally as part of government and commercial initiatives (Gill, 2017). As a result, academics report not only 'grave concerns about attempts to measure teaching quality' but

Neoliberalisation of the university 23

also 'changing student attitudes' (ibid.). When students are treated like consumers by the university, there is a strong likelihood that they will also behave like consumers.

The *Academics Anonymous* feature as part of *The Guardian* Newspaper has become an opportunity for academics to expose life in the neoliberal university. One incident reflects on a situation that describes a student who requested a tutorial to be held outside an academic's office hours. As the academic in question had missed a lecture due to illness, the student calculated the lecturer's absence to have cost her £160; thus, as she had missed out, the tutorial 'should take place when it suited her most' (Anonymous Academic, 2015). This is the ideal-type Homo economicus student that the neoliberals have intended to create. Another case that will be discussed in more detail later in this book is worth mentioning here because of its relevancy. During and after industrial strike action, some students sought compensation from their universities for their missed lectures and seminars, demonstrating that they have internalised the idea of being the consumer of goods. Acting with this consumerist financialised mindset is significantly symbolic in the way that the degree is consumed and seen as similar to any other commercially available commodity.

Technology

The continuous strive to revolutionise the process of production to widen markets to allow for further accumulation of capital has resulted in a constant drive for technological innovation. These innovations are crucial for the capitalist system as 'technological lead drives competition' and competition is one of the main components of neoliberal capitalism; not only does it allow the capitalists to increase profits, but it also disciplines the labourer 'under the threat of reconstructing or unemployment' (Hall, 2015c). In universities, utilising technology to control and discipline the labourer becomes increasingly easier as almost everything the academic does necessitates computers that can monitor actions. As academics can be monitored and their labour process has largely been automated, the academic labourer has become an 'appendage of the machine' (Marx and Engels, 2015, p. 12), which not only deprofessionalises the work itself, but also leads to increasingly proletarianised working conditions.

Technology, especially its recent advancements, plays a crucial role in the proletarianisation of higher education and academic labour, as it results in 'the degradation and deskilling of work under managerial control' (Woodcock, 2018, p. 131). Firstly, advancements in technology enable the globalised world to share information instantly, allowing countries to transcend previous boundaries (Olssen and Peters, 2005). Within the context of higher education, universities opening up campuses in other countries are an example. Often described with the terms like "going global", 'lecture capture' and 'digital learning strategies' enable institutions to branch out and sell their commodities in new markets (Harris et al. 2012, in Hall, 2017, p. 4). Utilising technology also allows for students to be taught fully through virtual learning environments and recorded lectures in the Massive Open Online Course initiatives (MOOC) (Rizvi, Donnelly, and Barber, 2013). As students can gain a degree without having to be present on campus, institutions save money on real estate, building maintenance, cleaning personnel, electricity, and more, as well as on academic staff's working hours. While this can be useful for students who have other commitments and are therefore unable to be physically present, the amount of fees often does not decrease although distance learning students are "cheaper" for the university to administer. Additionally, MOOCs can also be monitoring devices. They do not only entail control and surveillance of the student and the academic, which can lead to censorship in forums designed for open communication and discussion, they also leave academics vulnerable to scrutiny when their programmes do not generate enough "clicks" (Dehaye, 2016). Secondly, and most important in relation to the devaluing and deprofessionalisation of academic labour is the fact that academic labour is increasingly replaced by technology, such as with recorded lectures in order to save on academics' actual labour time (Hall, 2017). Accordingly, Hall (2013, p. 53) describes technology as a 'mechanism through which relationships, revealed through actions, emotions and affect, labour and service, are mined, closed-off and privatised, in order that they can be monetized'. The academics' focus has changed, no longer is the intellectual content most important, but rather the 'exchange-value that can be extracted' from the commodity produced by academics is prioritised (Hall, 2017, p. 3; Banfield, Maisuria, and Raduntz, 2016). Therefore, the number of publications, associated citations, and surveys assessing the satisfaction of students are used to evaluate academics' performance (O'Dwyer, Pinto, and McDonough, 2018) and institutions are able to use technology to monitor these metrics.

Ball (2000, p. 1) describes performativity as a 'technology, a culture and a mode of regulation ... that employs judgements, comparisons and displays as means of control'. Within the audit culture, performativity is increasingly used to monitor, evaluate, and judge the performance or outcomes not just of different institutions and departments, but also individuals. Hereby accountability is intensified, as academics find themselves under constant surveillance, which ultimately results in a loss of autonomy because he or she is constantly forced to meet targets or face the consequences (see Giroux, 2014). Accordingly, Ball (2003, p. 215) refers to the pressure as the "terror of performativity" and establishes that 'it does not simply change what people, as educators, scholars and researchers do, it changes who they are'. By 'creating new social identities', academics adapt to the mode of teaching that delivers the best outcomes, regardless of whether they believe it to be right (Ball, 2000, p. 2), as in this coercive environment 'you tend to value what is measurable, rather than measure what is valuable' (Boulter, 2011).

Exploring the role of technology in education, Hall (2015b, p. 107) highlights that 'technology is utilised by capitalists *both* to make labour more effective and efficient in the creation of commodities *and* to discipline labourers' (original emphasis). While monitoring through technology has increased with recent advancements in technological capability, the idea of monitoring workers is not new. According to Fulcher (2015, p. 7), the first 'silent monitors' were introduced at New Lanark mills by Robert Owen in the 1800s, where a piece of wood, with its sides painted in different colours indicating the 'quality of the previous day's work', was displayed in front of each worker and turned accordingly on a daily basis, in order to give an incentive to be more productive and the rewards were valued. The idea of monitoring was not designed to be punitive and Owen is described as the father of British co-operative movement (Ratner, 2012, p. 61), whose concern over the 'detrimental impact' of 'British industrialism' 'on working class people' led him to create 'worker-oriented factory villages with humanitarian oversight' (Hatcher, 2013, p. 414). Therefore, Owen was a socialist pioneer with his ideas of reducing their workers hours, improving education for his workers, and thus improving their general well-being. As Hatcher (2013, p. 416) demonstrates, Owen's ideas concerning the 'relationships between the nature of work and workers and between workers, managers and business owners' can be useful to examine the current conditions (which we do in Chapters 3 and 4). As collaboration, communication, and cooperation were clearly at the centre of Owen's ideas, one can only guess his reaction to the current developments, the (mis)appropriation of the modern "monitoring device", and the subsequent largely negative impact on workers today.

While, technology has been utilised by the capitalists to generate increasingly more income and to discipline workers, it has to be stated that technology is also available as an opportunity to build and materialise class consciousness, resistance, and class struggle.

The competitive academic

In the current era of neoliberal capitalism, competition is a crucial element that academics not only cannot avoid but are pressured to participate in. The situations of academics can be seen as a microcosm of class struggle.

26 Neoliberalisation of the university

Academics are employed by institutions and they are dependent on this employment in order to sustain themselves, which puts them into a vulnerable position where they are forced to compete with one another. Not only can they potentially be replaced by cheaper labour or technology at any time, but their role has also become one that is focused on applying for research-funding opportunities and publishing work that can generate revenue at a time when government funding is declining (Hall, 2017). All institutions conduct mock reviews, for example, for the Research Excellence Framework (REF) where academics' publications are reviewed by other academics in the department who are 'obliged to deliver graded verdicts', which does not only 'pollute collegial relationships', but it also 'constrains academic freedom' (Morrish, 2017). The culture and ethos that is being generated is dystopian. Discussing the consequences of competition between individuals in society, many years ago Engels (2009, p. 111) described it as 'a battle for life … fought not between the different classes of society only, but also between individual members of these classes', a quote which highlights the way that he (and Marx) proposed a differentiation between people in each of the two social classes; in our context, this points to the need for individuals to fend for themselves and be self-centred in order to assure as much job security as possible under the circumstances. This means that academics are divided, and so it is unsurprising then that these circumstances hinder organised trade union action and the working-class solidarity and collectivism that are needed to oppose their working conditions and neoliberalism more generally. As pointed out in *The Communist Manifesto*, the 'organization of the proletarians into a class, and consequently into a political party, is continually being upset again by the competition between the workers themselves' (Marx and Engels, 2015, p. 16).

While already competing with one another, the more qualified and experienced academics have to fear the reserve army, consisting of less skilled or perhaps lesser qualified staff that will cost the university less. Just as in any other business, more qualified and experienced labourers are more expensive. For a university that constantly seeks ways to drive down labour costs, employing those who require less pay would be seen as a viable option. This is especially true since in the neoliberal university 'academic labour' has largely been 'stripped of its intellectual content' (Hall, 2017, p. 3; Banfield, Maisuria, and Raduntz, 2016) and producing work of lower quality, or dubious ethics, is still permissible, as long as it pays. Less skilled and less experienced academics, hoping to make a career in academia and desperate for job opportunities and work experience most likely would not hesitate to take a job offered to them, even for little pay, for example, as hourly paid or on fractional contracts, putting the more experienced and qualified academics in danger of losing their jobs. This is also true for those academics who oppose the neoliberal conditions or whose 'goals' are 'not in line with those of their employer' and thus are considered a threat (Webb, 2018, p. 97); not toeing the line is a hazard. This issue of dispensability can be exemplified by the case of Thomas Docherty, a Professor of English and Comparative Literature who was suspended 'for giving off negative vibes' and 'inappropriate sighing' (Gardner, 2014), similarly and secondly is the case of Jeff Frank, Professor of economics, 'union activist' and 'dedicated equalities campaigner' (Dobinson, 2018). The grounds of Frank's suspension have been described as 'unreasonable and questionable' in a statement posted online on behalf of the UCU and RHUL branch committee (Royal Holloway UCU, no date). These cases of suspension are on allegedly dubious grounds. Although Docherty was able to resume his position after nine months, his case indicates that those who are "making life difficult" for the university are in danger of being disciplined. Additionally, there is the case of James Newell, a Professor of Politics, who was dismissed from his job for what Geoghegan (2018) tweets as 'insufficient contribution to the University's desire to strengthen its links with business'. These cases highlight reasons to believe that academics who reject the neoliberalisation of higher education have to fear the consequences, potentially even unemployment.

Considering the working conditions that academic workers face as a result of the configuring of academic labour, it is not surprising that many academics are overworked and suffer from mental and physical health issues. The late Professor Joyce Canaan, who co-pioneered Public Sociology in England and was fully committed to her role as an organic intellectual, was adamant that the neoliberalism inherent in her working life contributed to her heath declining and eventual demise (Canaan, 2016). Similarly, a recent and powerful case involved Dr Malcolm Anderson. The 48-year-old father and lecturer committed suicide, leaving a note citing 'work pressures and long hours' (BBC News, 2019). According to a BBC report of his death: 'He was dealing with over 600 students and on the day he took his life, in February 2018, he was in the middle of marking 418 exam papers, and preparing for a day of lectures' (ibid.). The article goes on:

> According to his wife, he was working evenings, weekends and holidays to keep on top of marking, preparing lectures, setting exam papers and answering emails. ... he was unable to take annual leave due to his workload in 2015, 2016 and 2017.

Dr Anderson's predicament was extreme but the pressurised conditions where near impossible quantities of marking, administration, bid-writing, and teaching are to be done, are common. Such is the naturalisation of exploitation in today's university, that some universities have introduced the idea of resilience training, which also appears on performance reviews. The idea is that if an academic cannot cope, it is an individual's failings and they need more steel, rather than it being a systemic and institutional problem. Unsurprisingly, many academics are forced to quit the profession altogether to avoid the kind of fates described above (Hall, 2017). This is reflected in a quote from the aforementioned Canaan (2013, p. 2) who lists a number of side effects of working in a neoliberal university environment:

> [E]xhaustion from overwork; performing a growing number of disheartening work practices; terror at the prospect of possible unemployment and growing fatalism as the attack on HE (higher education) is only part of a more pervasive government policy of privatising, marketising and financialising public service generally.

This phenomenon has given rise to "Quit Lit", a genre where academics write about the many reasons that have led them to quit academia. Resignation can be seen as signs of what Maisuria (2011, p. 288) describes as '"there is no alternative" fatalism', when academics feel that the toxicity is too deeply and widely entrenched, and they see no hope of professional and ethical practice remaining for them. Those who persist and stay within academia are increasingly alienated from their labour. This alienation is described by Bowles and Gintis (1976, p. 72) well before the current malaise in universities:

> The worker experiences this alienation in the form of powerlessness, meaninglessness, isolation, and self-estrangement. Powerless because work is bureaucratically organized, ruled from the top, through lines of hierarchical authority, treating the worker as just another piece of machinery, more or less delicate and subject to breakdown. ... Meaningless ... because the worker who produces goods designed for profit rather than human need realizes only too well how dubious is his or her contribution to social welfare.

Similarly, Hall (2017, p. 5) describes the cognitive dissonance that is needed in order for the academic to cope, on the one hand he or she needs to believe in and love what he or she does, while on the other hand being reduced to the exchange value of his or her work. This does not only increase the alienation from his or her work, but also leads to an alienation from personhood (Hall, 2017). Similarly, Moore (2009, p. 260) points out 'workers are expected to embrace their own alienation from their work and are told that the project of self-employability must become part of their subjectivity and self-worth'. As the academic labourer internalises the idea that he or she is only worth as much as the work he or she produces, the work eventually becomes more important than being human. This is what Hall (2017, p. 2) calls the 'self-exploiting entrepreneur' who is forced to sell herself 'piecemeal' (p. 4) in order to remain employable. In the words of Marx (2014, p. 82), 'the devaluation of the human world increases in direct relation with the *increase in value* of the world of things'; therefore, the more exchange value the academic creates, the more her own value decreases and he or she needs to work even harder, just in order to remain employed. Accordingly, it does not come as a surprise that the pressure academics are under becomes too much in certain cases. In addition to the Dr Anderson case discussed above, Stefan Grimm, a Professor of Toxicology took his own life in 2014 after being told that he was not bringing in enough research funding and thus was struggling to fulfil metrics (Parr, 2014, 2015). This and the Malcolm Anderson case are two examples that suggest the current lived reality of what Engels (2009, p. 111) referred to competition between individuals as a 'battle for life', could be read literally.

Employability and entrepreneurialism are important elements in an education system situated firmly within neoliberal capitalism. As Ford (2017, p. 455) highlights, there are two sets of people in education, the ones that '"can" and another set' that 'cannot'. Those who can are 'tasked with becoming self-entrepreneurs, constantly learning and relearning to meet the constantly shifting global market society' (ibid.), which, from a neoliberal perspective, can only be good for the economy. In this situation, the government's plan 'to shift responsibility for workers' welfare to workers themselves' is clearly visible (Moore, 2009, p. 265). Those who "can" are successful because they make necessary arrangements and do not shy away from change in order to retain their position on the labour market. Thus, it is unsurprising then that it has been made one of education's goals to train students for 'individual employability or entrepreneurialism of the self' (ibid.). Additionally, the idea of "flexibility" in this context becomes crucial and the term sends shivers down the spine 'of every worker today' (Fisher, 2009, p. 33). Being an entrepreneur in the current situation, being able to learn and relearn, requires flexibility as, in order 'to function effectively as a component of just-in-time production' workers 'must develop a capacity to respond to unforeseen events' and 'learn to live in conditions of total instability, or "precarity"' (ibid., p. 34). Mark Fisher, the author of this quote, is another fatality in academia after committing suicide aged 48.

As Peter McLaren discussed in the foreword to this book, faced with these already difficult conditions, some adjunct professors in the US do not even earn the minimum wage and have to rely on food stamps or a second job (c.f. Saccaro, 2014). Also, in the context of the US, O'Dwyer (2016) highlights that the academic's fear of unemployment does not only have a psychological impact but is also physically, emotionally, and financially draining. Saccaro (2014) observes that the majority of her colleagues are 'either overweight, living with mental illness, or … an autoimmune disorder', struggle to maintain relationships due to ongoing stress or regular moves 'interstate or overseas' and 'are financially worse off than their same aged, non-academic friends'. While these reports are concerned with academics in the US, decreasing pay and benefits, more work and less job security are also features of HE in England.

Curriculum

As a consequence of universities competing with one another, the curriculum has changed to maximise the potential of attracting students. This has meant a focus and prioritisation of employability and entrepreneurialism. Hall and Smyth (2016) point out that this change has wide-reaching consequences. They remind us that the curriculum shapes society by producing individuals whose ideas and values are shaped by the education they received. In a neoliberal capitalist system, this education perpetuates capitalist ideas and thereby universities 'produce highly individualized, responsibilized subjects' who have internalised the need for entrepreneurialism as well as competition and self-sufficiency (Davies and Bansel, 2007, p. 248). Additionally, the ties between universities and businesses have strengthened in recent years as universities increasingly had to "team up" with business in order to generate income. Encouraged by the government, universities should be open 'to involving employers … in curriculum design' (BIS, 2015, p. 11). As a result, worryingly for academic autonomy and professional ethics, businesses now have influence over curriculum content at many universities, meaning an embedding of the priorities of employers. Thus, it is not surprising that Porschitz, Smircich, and Calás (2016, p. 346) highlight that it is often business schools who partner 'with the private corporate sector in various ways including shaping their curricula to meet corporate employee standards'. However, the goal of the curriculum being 'simply employability' entails the 'risk of narrowing the curriculum to skills for work' where 'the concept of personal growth, or of development as "whole" individuals is lost' (Organisation for Economic Co-Operation and Development, 2002, p. 119). Additionally, this poses further problems for some disciplines and puts 'considerable pressure … on the arts, humanities, and social sciences' (Gillies, 2011, p. 238), which are increasingly pressured to prove their economic relevance (Nussbaum, 2010), a point that we discuss in more detail shortly.

Educational reforms implemented in times of political and social unrest often have hidden agendas, nefarious, and mendacious. One such example is the introduction of progressive education in the US between the 1890s and the 1930s. An expansion of secondary schools led to high schools' mass-producing graduates and with a new emphasis on flexible, child-centred education that takes into account students' ethnic diversity and surroundings; it was described as a 'radical new educational philosophy' (Bowles and Gintis, 1976, p. 180). However, while the transformation of secondary education 'from an upper class preserve to a mass institution was eminently consistent with democratic and egalitarian traditions', its close relation to corporate division of labour resulted in 'stratification and bureaucracy' instead of 'equality and democracy' (ibid., p. 192). Additionally, educational testing and tracking, which purport to encourage healthy and productive competition, in reality negatively impact the learning experience, and potentially can be very harmful to pupils (see Black and Wiliam, 1998; Boronski and Hassan, 2015; Gorlewski, 2016). Essentially, the goal of an 'integration of masses of new workers into the wage labour system' was achieved for economic benefit, 'producing a labour force for corporate enterprises' (Bowles and Gintis, 1976, pp. 180–181), this resonates with current education policy and reform, especially in the US (see Ryan, 2017, pp. 32–33). Wolf's (2002, p. 254) description of the consequences is fitting here:

Our preoccupation with education as an engine of growth has not only narrowed the way we think about education policy. It has also narrowed – dismally and progressively – our vision of education itself.

As 'the concrete work that teachers and students do inside and outside the classroom is subsumed under the compulsion to create and accumulate value', it leaves little space in higher education 'to become a social or communal good' or 'to address global socio-economic and socio-environmental crises' (Hall and Smyth, 2016, pp. 2–3). Accordingly, there is reflective concern among academics over how to do teaching for creating value benefitting not only the economy but also how to empower students to become active parts of the community that can think and act critically. Beckmann, Cooper, and Hill (2009, p. 311) state 'that the changes imposed in the name of "efficiency" are leading to the increasing production of uncritical thinkers' and leave little room 'for the provision of broad-based learning and critical awareness'. This is supported by Moore (2009) who suggests that the priority of any neoliberal government and governance of universities is not to educate individuals with knowledge and ability to think with critical reflectivity (e.g. articulating and synthesising neoliberalism to problems in lived reality) – what Giroux terms as 'connecting the dots'

(Giroux, 2016), but rather to produce individuals that are employable and exploitable, thus clearly focusing on growing the neoliberal economy. However, it is worth noting at this point that, in certain cases, criticality is welcomed by the neoliberal system, as long as it is within limits. Firstly, this is the case when said criticality benefits the neoliberal system by facilitating economic productivity. Secondly, criticality is also appreciated when being critical is confined to being conscious of sociocultural and economic political problems, such as inequality or climate change, as long as these are not attributed to neoliberalism or can be used to facilitate action against and thus challenge the neoliberal system.

Within many universities there is increasingly little room for genuine interdisciplinary collaboration. Several factors might be at work here. Firstly, it can be questioned whether academics have the time and energy to collaborate and share ideas with others while experiencing the multiplicity of pressures (discussed earlier) that will secure their employment. O'Dwyer, Pinto, and McDonough (2018, p. 244) point out that 'there is never enough time …, time is running out', and there 'is the pressure to produce more … that is measurable, … to produce more with less'. Secondly, the idea of departments competing with one another for funding might be another reason that inhibits academics from reaching out towards other disciplines; this is the malign impact of performativity. Corporate universities do not usually encourage sharing knowledge without the possibility of income generation. As pointed out by Hall and Smyth (2016), the structure of the curriculum also creates boundaries that are difficult to break. Considering the academic's fear of unemployment, it does not come as a surprise that he or she is less keen on interdisciplinary work with other departments whose success might mean his or her own loss. Again, this is the zero-sum game induced by neoliberalism engendering a mentality characterised by the maxim: "my loss is because of your win, and vice versa". Thus, the universities' attempt to discipline and control academics, preventing a possible collective resistance against increasingly exploitative conditions, has been achieved through the restructuring of the university and the internalisation of the narrative of all against all. To safeguard the neoliberal ideology, any collective action that could lead to critical reflection and potentially facilitate action against the system is negated. However, as Pereira (2016, p. 107) rightly points out, 'this is not the time for individual and isolated work within closed walls', there is much at stake, a point that we elaborate in Chapter 4.

Collegiality and collaboration have not been the only victims of neoliberal capitalism. 'Genuine creativity has been the greatest victim of new regulations as more rule-bound and quota-driven forms of competitiveness are superimposed on an already competitive profession', as a result 'universities have become "enterprises" to be managed by business principles, not by collegiality' (Fisher, 2007, p. 508). Donoghue (2008) points to another victim, the humanities, a discipline, broadly put, concerned with human society. Increasingly, departments struggle to 'justify their activities by pointing to the skills – in writing, reading, and expression – that humanities and social sciences emphasize' (Meranze, 2015, p. 1312). The nature of humanities and social sciences makes them unsuitable for league table comparison (e.g. for returns on pay), and they are not easily attributable to economic influence, making them, as Donoghue puts it, not "market-smart". Despite the importance of the arts, philosophy, or literature for questions about the nature of democracy, citizenship, and critical thinking, they are difficult to justify for a marketised arena focused on economic production. Martha Nussbaum highlights that 'economic growth does not invariably generate better quality of life', thus education should not solely be seen as 'a tool of economic growth' (Nussbaum, 2010, p. xi). She continues that teaching for economic growth results in educators ignoring subjects such as history, the arts and literature, as they pose a danger for the 'moral obtuseness necessary to carry out programs of economic development that ignore inequality' (p. 23), and might 'prompt critical thinking about the present' (p. 21) or question 'whether democracy can survive when huge inequalities in basic life-chances' exist (p. 20). Thus, Nussbaum (2010, pp. 20–21) concludes, 'critical thinking would not be a very important part of education for economic growth'; so, the humanities and social sciences are increasingly under attack in the neoliberal environment, and it is plausible that these attacks are motivated by a need to stifle critical reflectivity.

Moreover, the shape or form of the stifled critical reflectivity becomes relevant as not all critical thought is discouraged. As mentioned previously, in certain cases the neoliberal system permits criticality as long as it has some utility for sustaining itself. For example, universities permit and encourage criticality on parts of their academics as long as this criticality is accompanied by rising numbers of citations, publicity for the university, and/or potential research income opportunities. An academic who, although criticising the education system, regularly publishes papers, attends conferences, and thus generates interest in the university as well as "recruits" potential students who are interested in those critical approaches, still embodies worth for the university, albeit a questionable one.

3 Reality for new and prospective academics, and postgraduate students

Flexibility, transferable skills and the social sciences/humanities

In the previous chapters we have illustrated the changing of the role of the academic in recent years as neoliberalism has become more deeply and extensively entrenched in universities in a globalised economy. This restructuring has resulted in a proletarianisation of academic labour and in the alienation of academic labourers from their work. This is characterised by an increased pressure to meet targets, including an increasingly larger and more consistent generation of income expectancy, the deterioration of the academic profession, accompanied by mental health concerns and growing fatalism. Accordingly, it does not come as a surprise that these conditions seriously impact on university students and their relationships with academics and the university itself. This chapter will explore this context for the following groups of people: postgraduate students, and new and prospective academics – this includes hourly-paid lecturers, fixed-term contracted staff, and those including transferring from other sectors like further/tertiary and schools.

As described at several points previously, Marx discussed the necessity of the production of what he calls an industrial reserve army, a large number of workers who are available at any point to meet increasing demands of the economy – in academia, the prospective and new academics are those who are waiting to get a chance in an academic post. Prospective and new academics' unemployment is important for neoliberalism. The constant availability of these potential workers renders those employed, who are unsatisfied with their working conditions and who show signs of resistance, even though seemingly innocuous requests such as for fair payment for their labour, expendable, as the prospective and new academics will be readily available to take over the job. In many universities, graduate teaching assistants (GTAs), PhD students, new and prospective academics are commonly appointed to teach as well as supervise students in order for the university to save money. Therefore, more experienced and thus also more expensive academics are replaced by lesser experienced and lesser qualified staff for the sake of driving down labour costs (Hall, 2017). While this can be considered as valuable working experience for prospective academics, in neoliberalism the primary reason for their employment is that they are cheaper, more malleable to poorer working conditions, willing to comply with heavy workloads, and most probably non-unionised. This has not gone unnoticed. Questions are increasingly being raised of said "valuable working experiences", as according to Hall (2019), most doctoral students will not end up in academic careers and their teaching experience is ineffectual in securing employment. In relation to working conditions, they are employed without entitlement to holiday pay, sick pay, maternity/paternity rights, and compassionate leave. While these are basic rights, they cost money and the neoliberal university is bound to reduce outgoings. There are also important affective implications. In the neoliberal university, GTAs and PhD students are increasingly being asked to lead lectures, seminars, and even modules despite being underqualified and underexperienced. There is a strong possibility of a negativity impact on self-efficacy. In many cases, GTAs and PhD students, new and prospective academics are not adequately supported and nurtured to teach through mentoring by a more senior academic in the room – this would be costly and undermine the economic rationale for employing the junior in the first instance. Being dropped into a classroom, often with undergraduates of a similar age, and having to teach material that may be unfamiliar or has been designed by another lecturer, inevitably means that the individual will suffer anxiety and stress regarding their performance (see Jones, 2017). Additionally, they are very much aware of performativity (the need to show resilience) and that they are on trial – the calculation is simple: do well and be in line for a permanent job if one becomes available, do poorly and spend more time on the sidelines. The stakes are high. The main point is that the nurturing of up-and-coming academics has been lost to an economic imperative, and this is often disguised as building resilience and future capacity.

The drive for prudence in austere times has also impinged on universities' capacities to provide a supportive infrastructure for doctoral candidates. Stretched finances mean that only one supervisor is allocated per candidate, whereas previously it was a team of supervisors with varying specialist inputs. The reason for this change is that having one academic salary rather than two or three doing the same task is much cheaper. Reducing the size of supervisory teams means that academics can be freed up to do other tasks, such as bidding for external grants. This move reflects the move towards a business-type rationalisation for optimum financial productivity. It means that the nurturing of doctoral work becomes de-prioritised in the wider picture of university work. In this scenario, many academics are doing invisible work, such as providing advice and guidance on a regular basis without having institutional recognition and appreciation.

The previous chapter discussed changes to curriculum content, this section will extend that discussion elaborating on the notions of flexibility and transferable skills that prospective and new academics need to display. Being employable means having "generic skills" which 'are seen as *context-free*, abstracted from the circumstances of their formation and use, and freely transferable between sites' (Marginson, 1994, p. 8; original emphasis). This can be seen as an attack on developing disciplinary and subject-based knowledge. To explicate this point, Marginson cites a University Grants Committee: 'specific knowledge quickly becomes outdated', therefore universities should emphasise 'intellectual, scientific and technological principles rather than provide too narrow a specialist knowledge' (1994, p. 8). This statement was published in the 1980s, showing that flexibility for employability was encouraged from the beginnings of the neoliberal project. In this scenario, Marginson (1994, p. 8) concludes 'it seems that the seemingly timeless adage that "knowledge is power" has been replaced by "generic skill is power"'. However, opinions regarding transferable or generic skills differ and so Marginson refers to academics who have pointed out that 'skills such as critical thinking' are 'linked to particular knowledges' and certain skills usually found in 'the humanities and social sciences ... could only be learned and used in specific knowledge domains' (ibid., p. 12). Considering the current state of the social sciences it can be plausibly argued that these disciplines are in jeopardy precisely because they encourage powerful and empowering knowledge for building a platform for resistance to neoliberalism by, what we have in the previous chapter called critical reflectivity, which is about postgraduates (and others) articulating neoliberalism with problems in lived reality, for instance, their own future precarity.

At this point, it is useful to refer back to the writing of Nussbaum who argues for the relevance and even necessity of the humanities and social sciences as an essential element of education, which we extend to postgraduate training. She emphasises, for example, that being able 'to think well about a wide range of cultures, groups, and nations in the context of a grasp of the global economy' as well as understanding 'the history of many national and group interactions is crucial ... to enable democracies to deal responsibly with the problems' the nation faces (Nussbaum, 2010, p. 10). Thus, skills developed as part of a postgraduate degree in the humanities are also of economic benefit, as drawing 'on the humanities and arts' promotes 'a climate of responsible and watchful stewardship and a culture of creative innovation'; clearly, these are connected with productivity. Additionally, Marginson (1994, p. 24) points out that within the social sciences and humanities 'courses are characterised by more diversity in ways of seeing and thinking, by more attention to questions of values, than most other courses' and, as is noted, this way of thinking entails the ability to be flexible. This potential for flexibility is emphasised with postgraduate students who have developed critical skills and thus are able 'to see many dimensions of an issue' and be 'more flexible for a wide range of jobs' (ibid. p. 24), including, perhaps especially, academic jobs.

The precarious employment prospects in academia for postgraduates in the humanities and social sciences is often referred to as a crisis for their very existence. According to Meranze (2015), the government's growing interest for higher education to serve the economy is one of the reasons why the humanities and social sciences are struggling despite the arguments of people like Nussbaum and the numbers of enrolments being relatively stable. Additionally, as indicated earlier, questions are raised about whether stifling the humanities and social sciences might be motivated by political and ideological, as well as economic reasons. As Amsler (2010) suggests, the closure of the University of Middlesex's philosophy department, which 'was the universities best performing research unit' might be an example. Despite being 'recognised as "world-leading"' and having 'apparently contributed nearly half of their combined earnings from tuition and research to the university's budget', the department was closed (ibid.). Accordingly, it has been questioned whether 'the closure occurred at least partly because the philosophy department had hosted the progressive journal *Radical Philosophy*, which provided a critical voice to the neoliberalising agenda of those in power' (Maisuria, 2014, p. 292).

Taking this into account as well as considering the interests of the labour market discussed previously, there is an ethical dimension to emerge for experienced academics in relation to their postgraduates and GTAs. Humanities and social sciences continue to suffer because of limited resources and continued cutbacks. It is no surprise then that academics working within this field are beginning to actively discourage their students from pursuing a career in academia. This is partly to do with poor employment prospects (Hall, 2019) as well as ethics – knowing that academic life is often mistakenly delinked from neoliberal pressures. Discouraging students from pursuing a career in academia is a difficult decision to make. While the academic wants to see potential fulfilled and the discipline grow, the reality of life for a new and prospective academic is hard and there is a moral imperative to discuss this. Koukal (2010) refers to "the talk" he feels compelled to have with students who consider a postgraduate degree and career in a humanistic discipline:

> I tell my potential wisdom-seeker that ... though her studies have filled her with love of wisdom, she should think very carefully before making the serious commitment ... I tell her that securing a tenure-track position is unlikely, because today well over half of those teaching college-level classes in the United States are part-time instructors, with no prospect of tenure. These positions provide an abundance of teaching, but come with low wages, no benefits, no job security, and, more often than not, no office space in which to meet students. ... "You will in all likelihood be denigrated, exploited, impoverished, worked like a dog, and exiled," ... "If you insist on doing this, adopt the attitude of a saint to be martyred and do it out of the blind faith of love, because there are no rational reasons to pursue an advanced degree in the humanities".
>
> (p. 227)

Taking this example, the current situation does not only impact on academics themselves but also on the way they can encourage, or rather discourage, their students to pursue a postgraduate degree and a career in the humanities or social sciences. The nurturing element of academics' work has been disturbed by neoliberalism and academics are ethically compelled to tell of their own unstable existence, their precarious working conditions, and in certain cases of cognitive dissonance and mental health problems, which are likely to be exacerbated for the new and prospective academic. This is exemplified by Fazackerley (2019) in a report for *The Guardian* ominously entitled 'It's cut-throat': half of UK academics stressed and 40 percent thinking of leaving:

> Sally Le Page had planned to be an academic when she finished her PhD in biology at Oxford. She now makes science videos on YouTube, because she says the HE system isn't good for young academics' mental health.
>
> Le Page started getting depression and anxiety while doing her PhD. "All of my friends in Oxford were PhD students and I struggle to think of a single one who hasn't had depression or anxiety," she says. "It is a bad cocktail of factors that lead to mental health problems".

The kind of mental health problems that Le Page refers to is common in academia, particularly for the precariously employed new academic and also postgrad hoping to enter the profession. The article by Fazackerley (2019) states that 'Frequent rejection and a loss of control are making university staff isolated and ill'. She cites a study by the Education Support Partnership (ESP) into *Staff Wellbeing in Higher Education*. Here are some quotes from academics in the report (O'Brien and Guiney, 2019, p. 11)

> Personally, I feel that we have become separated and isolated. It doesn't feel like that when you are teaching but ploughing away on your own research can be really isolating. How does that impact on me? The sense of isolation can be very demoralising.
>
> If you are struggling mentally, say with anxiety, you feel like you are on your own unless you are lucky enough to have colleagues who care.
>
> My sense of isolation was further affected by some mental health issues – work comes in at set times – marking essays for example – and you just have to get them done by a certain date – regardless, it adds to being isolated.
>
> The community aspect of teaching and learning is going missing – it can be very lonely and not inclusive.
>
> Over the last 15 years I have seen things change a great deal – fear, an attack on autonomy, erosion of trust, isolation is now the norm.
>
> From where I stand, I see a divide and rule approach. No longer support the idea of team. Hierarchies exist that promote isolation of individuals.

These are damning description of working life in the university, and one quote stood out because he or she explicitly linked the alienation (Hall, 2017) inherent in academic work to neoliberalism:

> The system has changed. It used to be far more about the department, the team, but now it is more individualistic. Eventually all systems are at risk of disease. Individualism is one of the diseases in Higher Education. The result is that you become isolated, you feel isolated and this is not good for your sense of wellness.

If this is the way academics feel, the situation must be intensified for the new and prospective academic, especially he or she who is able to think with reflective criticality and can articulate the system's problems with neoliberalism.

Targets and mental health

One of the problems that the new and prospective academic will encounter is the pressure to hit performance targets. The ESP report (quoted above) draws attention to the affective dimension of 'The consumer model' of higher education, here are some of the views of the respondents in the research (O'Brien and Guiney, 2019, p. 12):

> In this consumer world of target after target that we are now in at universities, academics are under pressure and over-stretched.
>
> The problem with the target-driven system is that you always feel you are on the edge of being caught out. What for, you never know. It's a feeling that's there.
>
> The consumer model is seen as a generator of anxiety and pressure.
>
> You have to do all you can to keep student numbers high. Otherwise, next year one of your colleagues might lose their job.
>
> When I get time to reflect, I wonder how we ended up in a world where profit has become more important than pedagogy.

'Profit before pedagogy' is a regular theme in contributions to *The Guardian's Academics Anonymous* blog, the name of the blog clearly indicates the precarity of academics who require anonymity for safety reasons. In one of these articles, an academic describes his experience in a job interview, where he was told that his teaching credentials were less important than his 'experience as a consultant', as they were looking for '"instructors" with practical business experience', rather than someone with the ability to teach (Anonymous Academic, 2018b). In this case, there is no doubt that the students' experiences are impacted by the prioritisation of the business ethos, when their lecturers are chosen not for their ability to facilitate learning in the classroom, their teaching experience, and their knowledge, but for their ability to be businesslike. Entering this new job, the academic was surprised to hear that he would not be allowed to use his own teaching materials but that he would have to 'use the pre-established course syllabus' that, according to him, can be described as 'charlatanism, full of meaningless clichés and pseudo-vocational training' (ibid.). While the article describes the experience of an academic in the US, he points out that, after working in the UK previously, the UK is 'only a few steps behind' the US (ibid.) and recent developments in higher education institutions in England reflect this movement. Porschitz, Smircich, and Calás (2016, p. 246) point out how partnerships with private businesses impact education by 'shaping their curricula to meet corporate employee standards', which is only one indicator of being just behind the US. However, when describing his experiences, the academic also mentions the fact that his students agreed with his belief that knowledge should not be seen 'as just another market commodity' in the world of 'academic capitalism' (Anonymous Academic, 2018b). Thus, it can be argued that, instead of discouraging students, academics could draw on their students' ideas and encourage them to resist further neoliberalisation in solidarity with academics, from whichever side these students want to be on, outside or inside the university. In the words of Morrish (2017), 'If established academics feel threatened, imagine the vulnerability of a young scholar who is called to this kind of work', therefore students and aspiring academics in this corporatised education environment might be more in need of support, encouragement, and especially collaboration with more experienced academics than ever before – solidarity for a new kind of education system is foisted upon us. We delve further into this debate in the next chapter.

Another effect of the changes in higher education is that diversity in universities suffers. As Morrish (2017) highlights, while universities generally have policies that should support diversity as well as inclusion, the reality of the current structure is not compatible with these policies, as 'all researchers are now measured against the most exceptional, often unencumbered, scholars, regardless of individual location or ambition'. In this situation equality clearly suffers, aggravating the already precarious conditions that academics face, making it especially hard for new and prospective academics from disadvantaged backgrounds. This can also have an impact on postgraduate students. Often, university students who intend to do further study have to apply for funding in a similar way as academics; perhaps this is designed to be training. In order to be qualified for grants, a student has to prove "excellence", not only by producing grades above average but also by supplying references from suitably and appropriately credible academics, preferably the 'big names' as endorsement. In these situations, postgrad students, just like established academics, compete with one another, as funding is limited and apparently only "the best of the best" will be able to secure it. While this instils the idea of competition in postgrad students before they have fully stepped onto the path of becoming an academic, it also puts certain types of postgrads, due to personal circumstances and class background, at a disadvantage.

Earlier, we have alluded to the deterioration of mental health of academics, who have attributed this to the increasingly constant pressure to meet demands. This is exacerbated for new and prospective academics and postgraduates. Not only do PhD students exhibit more mental health problems than the general population and strategies for 'reducing isolation and increasing support networks' are necessary (Hall, 2019), but as a whole, the number of anxiety disorders and other mental health problems at university has increased and in the past decade the rate of suicides has nearly doubled (Marsh, 2017). For postgraduates and those new to the profession who have accumulated loan debt, there is increased pressure (ibid.). This is supported by Webb's (2018, p. 96) suggestion that postgrads 'experience higher education as an extended period of unpaid labor preparing them for an even longer period of crippling debt'. Another factor for declining mental health and increased anxiety in students might have to do with whether the student's decision to go on to postgraduate study is intrinsically or extrinsically motivated. Saunders (2007) highlights that 'goals can be intrinsic, good in and of themselves, or extrinsic, good in their ability to obtain something additional' (p. 5). In a reality where postgrad students, as customers, purchase education to enhance their human capital education turns into an extrinsic good, which, as a goal, is 'less personally satisfying and associated with excessive social comparison and unstable self-esteem' (Saunders, 2007, p. 5). Pairing this pressure of "social comparison" with the pressure of competition, and the prospect of tremendous debt, it is not surprising that students' mental health and well-being suffer. This situation may be more intense at more prestigious institutions. A prestigious university has recently been in the spotlight after ten students, 'a number of which have been confirmed as suicides', have died within 18 months (Weale, 2018a). One vice chancellor has indicated that mental health care may not be the responsibility of universities (Marsh, 2017; Weale, 2018b), and another university has developed a programme of developing mental wealth competencies in all its students as part of a career passport, presumably to be more resilient workers in a difficult context.

Others share the frustration regarding funding and criticise its distribution. With regard to this, Weale (2018a) states that at one university 'students are also increasingly irritated by the university's boast about spending an additional £1m on wellbeing services' while spending £300m 'on the university's new ... campus near the railway station, as part of a massive expansion programme'. This clearly aligns with universities' expanding programmes to accommodate an increasing number of students whose fees are considered necessary income. But additionally, it also reflects one *Academics Anonymous* contribution that highlights that students 'want their timetabling to work, their essays to be marked on time and their classes kept a reasonable size', rather than fountains, 'outdoor movie screens, permanent access to ping pong and giant chess' (Anonymous Academic, 2018a). Thus, the academic concludes, there is a disconnect between what the university thinks students want and what students need in order to flourish. However, shiny new buildings, 'gyms and touch screens' are better for advertising purposes, which is a crucial factor within the competitive landscape of education, as they can be shown in brochures and at open days (ibid.). Thus, funding would be available if it did not have to be spent on making the institution more marketable, but this possibility is undermined by universities' involvement in "academic capitalism". Universities prioritise marketing functions and income over mental health. For instance, universities are routinely recruiting doctoral students without the requisite criteria because they are a 'lucrative income stream' (Anonymous Academic, 2019). A whistle-blowing academic alleges that these students at their institution were also inadequately supervised because support and pastoral care were secondary concerns to income (ibid.):

> The international students recruited solely for income rather predictably did not make good progress because they were doomed to fail from the outset. Some of the research proposals were so poor as to be virtually illiterate, but they were still accepted so long as the students had their wallets open. ... Nobody cared about whether these students succeeded: they were provided with unsuitable supervisors who either didn't have a PhD or lacked expertise in the student's area of interest. I later discovered that some PhD students were not supervised at all. The computerised records claimed supervisions every one or two months, but the students said they took place once in two years. The quality of the work submitted at that point confirmed the students' version of events.

The academic goes on to allege that his whistle-blowing activity was repressed in the most serious manner and with severe consequences:

> I raised concerns about the practice verbally and in emails. A month later I was accused of gross misconduct (on another matter). I was accused of lacking professional integrity and taken through a shambolic disciplinary process. I received apologies but I was also advised to "shut up" about my concerns. The situation and how it was handled was devastating, and the stress became unbearable. The accusations of dishonesty were shocking and frightening, particularly as they were disseminated to other staff members.

The lesson to be learnt from this and others' experiences of raising concerns about the implications of financialisation and marketisation is that there will be serious consequences. Where once, academics assumed something like a surrogate role in nurturing the prospective academic and postgrad, now that relationship is different and damaged. Rikowski (2012) concludes:

> The student-as-consumer model is potentially a nightmare for HE. It cannot be assumed that staff / student relations can and will always become progressive and harmonious enough to rise above the antagonisms generated (increasingly) by the marketisation, commodification and capitalisation of HE in contemporary society.

44 Reality for new and prospective academics

While students and academics can work together within education to critique the situation, the current capitalised education system makes this difficult, not only do students fear a failure thereby rendering their investment valueless, they are also aware of the difficulties of finding a job after graduation and thus might abstain from joint action, in order to better their chances (ibid.). Neoliberalism has been successful in driving wedges between everybody in HE. Solidarity is trumped by competition, and fear of not measuring up.

The idea of a conflict of interest is reflected in responses to the recent strike action of academics over changes to the pension scheme. In early 2018, it emerged that academic staff at more than 60 UK universities would be faced with cuts that would impact their pensions and 'could leave them significantly worse off in retirement' (Zalewska, 2018), with almost £10,000 less per year (University and College Union, 2018a). As a result, the University and College Union (UCU) called for industrial action in the form of a 14-day strike to be taken (ibid.). As the strike proceeded, the responses of the students differed. While many students were committed in their support of their lecturers, others feared missing out on valuable teaching time, which had a perceived future monitory exchange value. While many students were 'turning up on picket lines, writing to their vice-chancellors, posting on social media and telling their lecturers that they support the pension strike' (Anonymous Academic, 2018a), one of the authors of this book (Helmes) was involved in informal conversations with students who were not supportive of the strike. It was revealed in these conversations that this absence of support was not due to the politics of the strike action, but rather that these students had come from overseas to study in the UK for only a year and thus, as non-European students paid a large sum of money for their studies. They felt their demands were not met by the university, who was expected to provide what they had paid for; thus indicative of a consumerist mindset. This example clearly reflects how some students have internalised the idea of universities primarily as providers of a commodity and themselves as customers. However, it can be questioned whether anyone can blame international students, who potentially do not have strong ties to the UK higher education system and who, for example, at the University of Sheffield, pay £16,800 for a postgraduate degree in education (University of Sheffield, 2018). The blame must be at the doors of the system.

An additional response of students to the strike action was a petition signed by 3,000 (Fyles, 2018) to 10,000 (Busby, 2018) students seeking compensation for missed lectures (numbers here vary depending on the source). However, considering the previously discussed tight budgets that universities are subjected to, compensating students might be more detrimental for institutions than students anticipate, especially for already struggling departments, when universities are forced to generate this money elsewhere (for example, through cuts or closures). As suggested in this book, those in the higher echelons of management acquiesce and manipulate the system to serve their own needs, thus they will most likely not save money in places where it hurts "their own"; put another way, workers are differentiated by class within an organisation – universities are no different from the cut-throat private sector in this regard. While the responses from students about strike action can be considered problematic for unifying resistance, the overall response of students has been positive and students have largely supported their lecturers in disputes. As the Anonymous Academic referred to earlier highlights, the strikes evoked an unexpected solidarity that shows 'the ability' of students to 'think critically' and can be 'a teachable moment' for educators as it challenges the 'assumption that if we treat students as consumers, they will act like consumers' (Anonymous Academic, 2018a). Additionally, saying '"no" collectively in the University' is also emphasised as a strategy of resistance by Hall (2017, p. 11). Thus, social solidarity offers a glimmer of hope in the marketised and financialised landscape of higher education.

Early career academics

Building on previous sections of this chapter where the experiences of GTAs and prospective academics were explored, the following section will focus more extensively on the experiences of those who have just entered the profession as new academics, in literature often described as early career academics (ECAs), their position within the university, the ethical dilemmas they face when entering a system that seeks to: restrict their autonomy, stifle their creativity, and their quest for establishing an academic identity. However, it has to be noted that the term ECA is not well defined, generally however, it refers to 'academics in the early stages of their career' (Sutherland and Taylor, 2011, p. 183), and includes all academics within ten years of taking up an academic position in the university or completing a doctorate. While they are one career step ahead of GTAs and PhD students, their situation is not any less precarious and comes with its own struggles, difficulties, and ethical dilemmas.

For many ECAs, stress becomes omnipresent. Difficulties in finding a work-life balance, lack of real and effective support and mentoring, anxiety, little job security, and disillusionment are frequently mentioned by ECAs when asked about their experiences (Acker and Webber, 2017; Bristow, Robinson, and Ratle, 2017; Eddy and Gaston-Gayles, 2008). While it should be noted that these difficulties continue to impact academics that are more experienced, ECAs are especially vulnerable 'and the first to succumb to the pressures of the system' (Bristow, Robinson, and Ratle, 2017, p. 1186). Additionally, ECAs' contracts are more likely to be short-term contracts and/or require them to regularly relocate, a point that Macfarlane picks up clearly in his analysis of academic curriculum vitarum as a barometer of the changing nature of academic life with respect to performativity and managed marketised self-promotion, that show multiple moves before an ECA settles, relatively at least (McAlpine, 2012; McLachlan, 2017; Macfarlane, 2018). Continuously looking for a new job for after yet another short-term contract has ended or moving to a new city or even country becomes a necessity and requires ECAs to constantly transition their academic identity and to be "flexible" enough to adapt to a new working environment time and time again.

As touched upon previously in this chapter, postgraduate students are eager to teach while studying, especially those who see themselves entering into an academic career after their studies. Knowing this, universities are able to use this to their advantage. Not only does employing postgraduate students to teach, grade, and supervise save the institution money, but it also eases postgraduate students into the neoliberal education system that seeks to stifle any thought that might jeopardise the academy's status – being grateful is part of the job for many ECAs. The possibility to "prepare" those who will be ECAs in near future and save money at the same time means the neoliberal university can kill two birds with one stone, a chance that cannot be missed. Furthermore, these students are not only rewarded financially, albeit with poor renumeration, but also with the belief that their teaching experience will be valuable once they apply for academic positions. As mentioned previously, this is contested, as the majority of PhD students will not be able to work in academia after all (McAlpine, 2012; Hall, 2019), as the job market seems permanently limited and more people than ever have PhDs. Thus, taking up a teaching position as a postgraduate student without much prospect of securing a long-term teaching position later on might give these students a false sense of security, even entitlement. Additionally, as pointed out by Ball (2012, p. 19), where performativity is concerned, 'experience is nothing, productivity is everything'. Therefore, being productive (read: producing work for publication or bringing in research grants), is prioritised, even 'at the cost of being critical' (McLachlan, 2017, p. 65), and, as noted by the Anonymous Academic previously, being an experienced teacher does not account for much if it does not align with an institution's corporate statement.

As mentioned before, degrees such as those in the humanities and social sciences are at risk not only because they seldomly show to directly impact the economy and also because they allow students to develop skills to think about a broad range of topics with criticality, thus posing a potential threat for the neoliberal university. However, for the ECAs who have developed these skills as students and decided to pursue a career in academia afterwards, this has further implications. This is not only the case for the humanities and social sciences but for all degrees that originate in critical theory as the values and ideas students develop throughout these degrees are often times incompatible with the business ethos of the university. For example, Bristow, Robinson, and Ratle (2017, p. 1186) discuss their experiences of studying Critical Management Studies and explore the tensions that arise when ECAs become 'resisters and participants in the complex and contradictory forces constituting their field'. While their degrees enable them to become critical and thus equip them with tools to become resisters, they nevertheless become part of the system when they begin to establish the publication record that is necessary for their career. Even if their published papers are written with criticality, the authors become complicit in the 'system they set out to challenge' (ibid., p. 1190). Thus, prospective academics or ECAs who know the "rules of the game" and use this knowledge to their advantage, ironically play into the hands of the neoliberal system by participating in it. This shows the compromised situation of ECAs, who, despite their best efforts, are obliged to play into the hands of the neoliberal university in order to become "successful academics".

As Bristow, Robinson, and Ratle (2017, p. 1189) point out, precarious working conditions, 'immense pressures to perform', and the ever-increasing demand of the job lead to academic identity being 'fundamentally insecure'. This leaves ECAs in a liminal state with their values that in many cases are the reason for their pursuit of a career in academia, and the neoliberal ideology of the university setting. Despite ECAs starting out with an eagerness to resist the current neoliberal higher education system, many of them struggle to come to terms with their own complicity in the system they detest. This 'conflict', according to Smith (2017, p. 601), 'has the potential to disempower', as 'framing appropriate ambitions' under these conditions can be a challenge and thus 'can have a destabilising effect on' the ECAs' personal and political identity. McLachlan (2017, p. 66) points out that she was expected 'to reinvent' herself 'from a critical scholar ... invested in grappling with long-standing, complex social and cultural problems' to fit into 'the uncompromising conditions' of the neoliberal university. Although referring to all academics and not ECAs in particular, Loick (2018, p. 233) highlights 'the contradiction between the ideals of critical theory and the reality of academic practice'. He refers to academics becoming complicit in reproducing the same 'kinds of oppression they criticise' when they begin to grade students' 'papers according to predefined standards' 'and push them to complying with hegemonic' ideals (ibid.). In this case, the educator becomes what Isomöttönen (2018, p. 870) calls a 'degree system representative' rather than a critical scholar, researcher, and teacher.

Even those who enter academia with enthusiasm to make a difference in the divided system that they have become critical of as students, quickly find themselves buried under never-ending bureaucratic tasks, ever more marking and filling in applications for grants and external funding. Most likely neither of these tasks is the reason why an individual decided to work in academia, but they take up valuable time and energy regardless. Additionally, being a new member of staff also results in ECAs being exposed to increased surveillance (Smith, 2017) and, in many cases, they have to undergo regular reviews. Therefore, ECAs do not only have less time to invest in seeking ways to resist the system, but also to pursue their own interests and ideas regarding research and teaching. As a result, ECAs struggle to find meaning in their work. McLachlan (2017, p. 59), for example, questions whether it is possible to 'carry out lengthy philosophical inquiries that have no immediate reward or output' or to engage in meaningful research 'that might benefit disadvantaged or marginalised lives rather than meet the CV expectations of hiring committees', this is the empirical reality of a system where success is measured only by what is measurable, preferably immediately.

At this point, it should be mentioned that additional problems arise for certain minority or underrepresented groups, especially from working-class backgrounds. According to Ward and Wolf-Wendel (2004), women find it especially difficult to combine working within academia and starting a family, and Eddy and Gaston-Gayles (2008, p. 98) report that when asked, male academics found their roles to allow for 'more family time', whereas some female academics described the 'pressures they face balancing a family and academic work', suggesting discrepancies between the experiences of male and female ECAs, especially those planning to have a family. While this is not only a problem for ECAs, their even more precarious position intensifies their disadvantage. Furthermore, it can be argued that the majority of ECAs start their careers at an age when they also consider starting a family, inevitably making this a more common issue. Another group that experiences increased pressure, are academics from Black and Minority Ethnic backgrounds. Due to their under-representation in academia, they are often expected to 'fill multiple committee roles to have a diverse representation for these groups' and 'serve as mentors for students of color' while feeling they have to be especially 'friendly and accessible to people' as the 'spotlight' is on them more than on other new faculty members (Eddy and Gaston-Gayles, 2008, p. 97).

Taking these points above into account, it is not surprising that a 'sense of disillusionment' with academia is a common side effect for ECAs (Bristow, Robinson, and Ratle, 2017, p. 1186). When asking senior academics for guidance on how to challenge the existing system, McLachlan (2017, p. 65) was told she was hanging on to a 'somewhat romantic version' of academia. Unsurprisingly, concerns have been raised about the lack of socialization that ECAs receive when first entering the university as staff after finishing their graduate programmes. While graduate programmes are considered preparation for future employment in academia, 'the socialization process often is not very thorough' and thus 'may contribute to significant stress' for ECAs (Eddy and Gaston-Gayles, 2008, p. 91). There seems to be an assumption that an individual emerges from a PhD as a fully fledged academic, a 'highly trained researcher', 'more than ready to become an efficient, productive member of the academic workforce' (McLachlan, 2017, p. 65).

While mentorship by senior academics has been highlighted as a crucial factor for well-being, development, and adjustment of ECAs in their new roles (Monk and McKay, 2017), it is plausible that the constant demand put on senior academics, as well as their growing fatalism towards the academy, especially in certain disciplines, is to blame for their incapacity to fully support and mentor new staff. While certainly enjoying more stable conditions than ECAs, for those who have been in the profession for a while, the previous 'year's efforts' become 'a benchmark for improvement – more publications, more research grants, more students' (Ball, 2012, p. 19); thus, the demand to be more "excellent" this year than last never ceases. Furthermore, existing power dynamics between ECAs and more senior staff cannot be forgotten. While academics consider themselves open to new ideas, it can be difficult for new academics to disagree with the work or understanding of someone who has been in the profession much longer. Especially in collaborations, this can be a problem when co-producers' values or beliefs differ and the ECA most likely does not feel confident to raise an issue. Instead, they might resort to "waiting this one out" and include issues they find worth exploring in work they produce at a later stage in their career, when they are more established. In any case, ECAs not receiving the desired and necessary support and guidance from more senior academics, or possibly even receiving guidance that affirms neoliberal ideas, can be described as one of the reasons why the 'present social and political order' of the current education system 'is something that its subjects take to be inevitable' (Davies and Bansel, 2007, p. 247).

Monk and McKay (2017, pp. 226–227) propose that with the appropriate support network, even the 'unstable' identity of ECAs is not experienced as 'problematic and insecure', rather it is seen 'as simply responsive to the context of the moment', something that will not last forever but is part of the process. This presents existing support networks as ever more crucial. Besides support from senior academics, there are a number of other factors that are considered to benefit ECAs. For example, Bristow, Robinson, and Ratle (2017, p. 1193) highlight that ECAs can take advantage of their status as the "newbies" by questioning processes, or ' deliberately using or feigning naivety as a pretext for doing things that are not meant to be done', and their research suggests that ECAs can and do employ various strategies to do so. While Acker and Webber (2017, p. 546) highlight an ECA's account that 'rocking the boat' as an ECA is 'truly not a good idea' because of 'the potentially serious consequences' that could blight or end one's career, Bristow, Robinson, and Ratle (2017) suggest that trying to exclude ECAs from resistance movements or advising them to leave criticising the establishment to those who are more experienced and closer to retirement, is likewise problematic. This approach frames ECAs as passive and weak instead of having agency to resist, it does not only negatively affect their self-confidence and worth but also their status within the faculty and should therefore not be encouraged. Additionally, there are further implications if those senior academics, who the criticising and resisting is left to, have internalised neoliberal ideals or have become fatalistic.

According to Monk and McKay (2017, p. 226), building communities, small networks consisting of other ECAs, can provide 'a space to make sense' of the setting in which ECAs are developing their academic identities. This would allow them to reflect on and affirm those 'competencies that had initially brought [them] to [their] new academic positions' (ibid.). However, it has to be acknowledged that, while a universal problem, some countries' higher education systems are more impacted by neoliberal policies than others, nevertheless, the sense of insecurity exists everywhere. In Canada for example, emerging academics start their career as Assistant Professors, a position generally held for five or six years, so perhaps already much longer than most ECAs in the UK can hope for their appointment to last (Acker and Webber, 2017). At that point, after a successful review, although 'extensive and labour-intensive', usually leads to tenure and a position as Associate Professor (ibid., p. 543). Despite this relative safety, compared to that of ECAs in the UK, and being well-paid and protected by strong academic unions, 'pre-tenure academics [are] struggling anxiously with the opaqueness of tenure guidelines' (Acker and Webber, 2017, p. 544). While expectations to obtain 'external grants' and 'accumulating high-prestige publications' have increased for all academics in Canadian universities (ibid. p. 543), ECAs 'simultaneously need to hone in their teaching skills' (p. 544), while developing their identities as new academics. Thus, although ECAs in Canada enjoy more security than their UK counterparts, their experiences are similar.

Reality for new and prospective academics 51

In a neoliberalised landscape, it is worth reiterating that conditions for ECAs are especially precarious. Described by Acker and Webber (2017, p. 551) as 'resembling a made-to-measure product', ECAs have to come to terms with their own complicity in the neoliberal education system, increasing demands, incessant need to meet targets and to reinvent themselves. As a result, they experience disillusionment and alienation where 'the connection that the labourer experiences to work is lost' when their work is commodified (Sutton, 2017, p. 632). While there are some supportive factors that can alleviate ECAs access and facilitate adjustment to life as an academic in the current climate, the scope for resistance, especially at this stage of career, is limited. Unfortunately, those who are most critical of the system and desperately want to challenge its neoliberal structure, are also often those academics who leave the profession because they can 'no longer bear the contradiction between the ideals of critical theory and the reality of academia' (Loick, 2018, p. 234). The wedge is deep and fatalism often prevails, the beginning of the preface to this book is testament.

4 Struggle for a new reality

Feasibility of the emergence of alternatives

This book is part of the growing field of Critical University Studies (CUS), which according to Roberts (2017, p. 1) 'employs history, sociology, economics, and political science to analyze the ways higher education is being shaped by larger cultural forces'. Therefore, CUS authors such as Rustin (2016), seeks to draw attention to neoliberal policies, especially corporatisation, that impact on higher education and result in structural inequalities that create lived realities. The aim for CUS scholars is to 'maintain academic dignity, freedom, justice and integrity in this volatile occupation we call higher education' (Petrina and Ross, 2014, p. 62). The proliferating literature indicates significant interest and suggests an attitude far removed from fatalism associated with TINA (There is No Alternative). While Roberts (2017, p. 3) acknowledges that there will most likely not be 'a Department of Critical University Studies', the 'production of scholarship and practices that resist traditional university structures' is nevertheless apparent and clearly contributes to what Webb (2018, p. 97) describes:

> The university is recognized increasingly as a corrupt and criminal institution complicit in patriarchal, colonial and racist systems and processes; a criminal institution comparable to the police as a racialized, gendered and class-based force of authority, surveillance, enforcement and enactments of everyday patterns of structural violence.

While various scholars highlight that 'higher education never went through a golden era when knowledge was pursued solely or even primarily for its own sake' (Canaan and Shumar, 2008, p. 1) and according to Webb (2018) many academics paint a romanticised fairy-tale picture of the postwar university, it is important to acknowledge that the current conditions are worse than they have been prior to the restructuring of education under neoliberalism.

Struggle for a new reality 53

There is a clear necessity for envisioning a possibility for change. The Italian communist Antonio Gramsci viewed that it was necessary for the masses to have a new *conception of the world*, thus meaning that people must be convinced to believe that history is open to new ways of manifesting (Gramsci, 1971, p. 465; Forgacs, 2000, p. 429). In recent times, it seems that a consciousness is emerging amongst the labouring classes, including almost all academics, that there must be an alternative to the status quo because the way things are, are unsustainable in every way. Academics have endured gradual and piecemeal regression of their autonomy and freedom, as well as seeing the conception of the university change to be now about business and economic productivity accompanied with poor mental health implications, rather than individual and societal flourishing. For many years, dominant hegemony has been created by the appearance of having academic freedom that acts to obscure reality (Maisuria, 2017b), but as neoliberalism deepens, this appearance is being unveiled and demystified with declining salaries (real-terms) and the worsening of working conditions. The prevailing consciousness among most academics has been that relative favourable pay and conditions are what differentiates them from most other workers, but this appearance is also wearing thin.

The neoliberal status quo has been reproduced and deepened over many years via a general apathy towards change being feasible (Maisuria, 2017b), and also an increase in competitiveness that negates solidarity, organisation, and unity; all of which emerges in a fatalism taking hold. However, the emerging problem for neoliberals is that the previously apathetic masses are seemingly more aware of their inaction against the neoliberalisation of universities and academic work, and apathy is changing. This change has emerged out of necessity, and also the struggle for change being fought for by academics themselves, trade unions, students, and also politicians, all using their consciousness, ethics, and acting with what Gramsci called, their organic intellectualism to create and activate a different dominant hegemony. This move can be contextualised more widely with the massive support of Jeremy Corbyn's Labour Party, which has grown to be the biggest political organisation in Europe. Corbyn has been sharply critical of the inequality in society, and his vision for the National Education Service has invigorated hope for an education system that has been described as being in crisis (see Maisuria, 2019). In our view, all academic workers need to engage with and commit to the proposed NES and see the proposal as a route to consciousness for creating a feasible framework, which, while working within neoliberalism, would simultaneously be building the capacity for resisting and replacing it.

Towards the National Education Service (NES)

A fully comprehensive and unified Nationalised Education Service would be a radical break in recent history. It counters the increasingly prevailing idea that university education is an investment for the individual and therefore that the individual should be prepared to be financially indebted for the rest of their life. This dominant idea that effectively renders higher education a commodity is reversed with the NES idea that everyone through higher and more progressive taxation should pay for tuition-free universities because a highly educated society not only benefits the individual, but it also makes society. The NES proposal is to broadly mirror the original principles that underpinned the creation of the National Health Service in 1945. In summary, these principles were:

- Free at point use
- Accessible to everyone
- Taxpayer funded
- Common good / public service status
- Not subjected to market forces
- A mass and unified system
- All through – from cradle to grave

As well as fairness, the Labour Party Manifesto of 2017 makes the straight analogy between the establishment and the original principles of the NHS (importantly, these are in tension with the current semi-privatised NHS) and the proposed NES:

> When the 1945 Labour Government established the NHS, it created one of the central institutions of the fairness of the twentieth century. The NES will do the same for the twenty-first, giving people confidence and hope by making education a right not a privilege and building bridges.
> (Labour Party, 2017)

The Manifesto makes explicit that the purpose of education should be reconfigured to be about creating a culture of collectivity:

> When... [education] fails, it isn't just the individual that is held back, but all of us. When we invest in people to develop their skills and capabilities, we all benefit from a stronger economy and society.
> (Labour Party, 2017)

There are significant implications for university workers here because the NES is a proposal to pull back from close to 40 years of marketisation and

Struggle for a new reality 55

commodification in higher education. There has never been a revolution of the whole system like this, and the aspiration and scale of the task is phenomenal. It is therefore important to emphasise the deployment of the word "Towards" in the title: *Towards the National Education Service*. It is a crucial nuance that signifies the recognition that changes will manifest gradually, but the point is to redirect education policy away from neoliberalism. An adequately funded universities sector would mean that there is less emphasis on league tables and marketing the university like for-profit companies, and importantly that academic workers would be working within a new ethos.

This new ethos in the NES would come through several changes to recent manifestations, including trust, professionalism, and democracy – all in the service of the university as a public entity for the many. This new ethos must be struggled for, there is no prescriptive blueprint for this new university system, it would not be a top-down highly centralised system beyond establishing and protecting principles. It would be a collective and localised endeavour – academic workers are in the best position to provide leadership for a new conception of the university and its work. In this vein, we borrow from the Universities and Colleges Union De Montfort University branch (DMU UCU, 2019), which has established a series of principles guided by the International Co-operative Association:

1   Governance at the University will be based on active participation open to all its staff and students, based on democratic principles. This will be without any form of discrimination.
2   All staff representatives must be directly elected by staff. Those serving as elected representatives are accountable to the staff and student body first and foremost.
3   Decision-making must be predicated on the autonomy and independence of the University, and its staff and students. Where the University enters into agreements with other organisations, including raising capital from external sources, it must maintain the institution's focus on democratic principles and autonomy.
4   The University will demonstrate Concern for Community, including working for the sustainable development of its communities through policies approved by their members.
5   All those elected must adhere to the Nolan Committee's seven principles of public life: selflessness, integrity, objectivity, accountability, openness, honesty, and leadership in demonstrating the other principles.

While these principles for the ethos of the NES may sound non-revolutionary, they are in fact a radical change from the current trajectory. At the heart of many of the principles is the struggle for a new type of governance.

The university has descended into a situation characterised by mistrust. Academics often feel vulnerable because of intense competition to perform and get favourable metrics; this is a climate of fear of solidarity and collegiality. As Macfarlane (2016, p. 31) notes, this also has implications on the way that new, emerging, and prospective academics are nurtured:

> Collegiality is one of the most symbolically significant concepts of higher education and continues to be widely espoused as a core value by members of the academic profession. However, the highly competitive and performative nature of modern higher education means that the conventional values and behaviours associated with collegiality, such as mentoring and consensual decision-making, are coming under increasing pressure.

Academics mistrust the university management especially the higher echelons. There is a feeling among academics that management is more on the side of capital than labour. In practice, this has meant that Governing Boards' and Vice Chancellors' decisions have not been led by consultation with staff and students, rather they are indicative of the commercialisation of the university sector, for example, sponsorship by technology companies who will lead on designing teaching material and pedagogy, and subsidiary companies supplying cheap and exploitable labour. Regarding the latter, in October 2014, UCU "conducted a Freedom of Information [FoI] request which revealed that 61 colleges and 64 universities already made use of subsidiary companies to deliver teaching" (UCU, 2016). The fact that FoI was needed to glean this information suggests a serious deficiency in transparency. To address this, academics should respond with a demand for direct democracy and an equal (in numbers and weighting) voice in governance as part of an NES. Again, we borrow from DMU UCU to provide some practicalities:

- The Board of Governors, Executive Board, Academic Board, and all relevant sub-committees should seek to be as representative as possible of the diverse communities that [the University and its academics] serve. This includes democratic representation of at least two members from each recognised trade union.
- Increase democratic governance such that all staff can have an official voice through the creation of a General Assembly. Staff from this Assembly to be elected to all Governance committees of the University.
- Democratise all Governance committees and sub-committees through the allocation of equal votes to staff and student representatives, community members, and employers' representatives. ... Elect chairs of [all]committees. ... Full, transparent publication of all Committee and sub-committee minutes.

Struggle for a new reality 57

The fight for democracy and representative governance will be a long one given the depth of neoliberalism in the operation of the once public university. Recently, a notable success was recorded by academics at Coventry University where a subsidiary company of the university was handed union representation by management for its academic workers. This initial managerial move happened without the consent of the workers, who led a campaign to have UCU restored to represent them instead of the "sham union". The sustained and committed action of staff involved local MP Jim Cunningham who took the issue to a debate in Parliament, stating (Coventry Observer, 2018):

> I am appalled that an institution as well respected as Coventry University would use a loophole in Trade Union Law to register a Staff Consultative Group as a Trade Union solely to prevent having to recognise a bona fide Trade Union like UCU.

After five years of struggle, UCU (UCU, 2018b) released the following statement about the Coventry University Group (CUG, the subsidiary company):

> CU Group and the University and College Union are pleased to announce that they have today concluded negotiations and signed a voluntary recognition agreement. Under the agreement, UCU will be recognised to negotiate for academic staff at the company's three campuses.

The success of Coventry University workers provides hope and exemplifies success with struggle. It was clear that a business-led approach was antithetical to its workers, and industrial relations came to an impasse. DMU UCU (2019) proposes a different model of financial management based on ethics and values different from purely/primarily economism:

- Finance of the institution needs to be brought into the democratic realm such that [everyone] can analyse its processes and contribute to its planning.
- Openness and transparency about where and how decisions are made, where responsibility lies and clarity about how decisions may be questioned and challenged.
- A reconnection between the governance/policy of the University and its economy through democratic engagement with staff and students, so that economic value does not drive the approach of the University to its public role or generation of wealth.
- A commitment to ethical investment decisions.

58 Struggle for a new reality

We propose that academics stridently recommend these to be at the heart of the NES to combine financial responsibility and accountability with transparency and openness.

A specific area of concern for the NES must be the nature and content of teaching and learning. Ideally, teaching ought to be highly interactive, creative, exploratory, risky, and student-centred, but instead it has become a part of strategic thinking to game, thus to maximise the chances of reaping metrics, namely in the Teaching Excellence Framework (TEF) and the National Student Survey (NSS), both are supposedly objective and nationally administered measures of excellence of teaching. The centrality of the TEF and NSS in the life of the academic cannot be overstated. This is despite being devoid of real meaning for students when making choices about the TEF and NSS which university to apply to, and widely acknowledged to be spurious indicators of excellence.

Some historical overview is important here. Beginning in 2015, the government at the time suggested three ways (which became six in 2017 – as discussed below) that excellence can be measured.[1] One of the initial three ways that excellence as part of the TEF was to be evidenced, was student evaluation questionnaires, particularly the National Student Survey (NSS). The NSS is (voluntarily) undertaken by all final year undergraduates and the results are then published online by Unistats, where courses can be compared using Key Information Set (KIS) data, such as employment prospects. The usefulness of this is very ambiguous. In neoliberalised conditions where there is a dominant narrative focusing on investing in a degree to justify the circa £57k debt (Institute for Fiscal Studies, 2017), it may seem plausible and reasonable to create metrics to measure the quality and standards of degrees and their outcomes. However, there have been several extremely problematic consequences attached to the TEF and NSS. One such consequence is grade inflation, a term used to describe the increase in awards of higher classification degrees. The experience of the NSS for many academics is that "awarding" students 2:1 or first-class grades reap more positive responses on student satisfaction evaluations. Equally, academics will anecdotally reveal that even if students have had a deeply enriching, interesting, and insightful learning experience, they will still express dissatisfaction if they do not get a 2:1 or a first because these are the entry requirements for degree-level jobs. As well as the learning experience being reduced to measurable outcomes, i.e. whether or not a first or 2:1 is the award, evaluations are sometimes more indicative of the academic's personality and/or character, rather than a measure of excellence of teaching and learning. Academics who are approachable and flexible (perhaps open to reading several drafts of work, extending deadlines, being lenient, and so forth), even entertaining and funny (rather than, perhaps,

Struggle for a new reality 59

challenging, serious, and demanding), are more likely to satisfy students and would score more highly in judgements of excellence. Equally, wider issues apply, such as preferable class start time, high-quality classrooms and facilities such as the plentiful availability of library resources. The point here is that student evaluations, such as the NSS, are at best spurious instruments for measurements of excellence, and they are high stakes for the academic worker in the context of the importance of performativity, especially for the new(er) academic who is on probation.

For the second TEF metric part of the initial introduction, excellence was to be measured on retention of students and continuation rates (this is the number of students who pass their modules/year/course of study and, ultimately, complete their programme at the first attempt). Here again, there is pressure on academics to pass students rather than award deserving fails, especially marginal fails. Widening participation universities will be implicated the most. These universities attract nontraditional students who are almost always from working-class backgrounds and will not necessarily start university with the academic skills-set needed to progress at the first attempt. In addition, these students may often have additional personal and private challenges to deal with that impact their academic performance, for example, coping with the consequences of austerity (food poverty, homelessness, care-responsibilities), which may mean that they have to leave university to simply stabilise their life. The point is that the stakes are high for academics, who will be pressurised to: (i) award higher than deserved grades to high-quality academic work; (ii) pass academically poor-quality work that is a borderline fail to maximise the potential for a good score on student evaluations of excellence/pass rates; and (iii) to give the benefit of the doubt to the 2:2/2:1 borderline student. There is increasingly a comfort zone consisting of awarding mid range grades, away from borderlines, which is "encouraged" by management.

The third metric that was proposed to contribute to the TEF in the initial plans was a measure of what graduates go on to do after leaving university (graduate employment and destination). Once again, the issue of grade inflation arises, whereby a graduate with a 2:1 or a first is much more likely to get a "good" job, which is about salary. Like the NSS metric, again, academics are being pressurised to award 2:1 and first-class degrees to improve their students' chances to get a "good" job to score well in this measure. The TEF induces grade inflation that will, in turn, likely test the professional integrity and ethics of academics. The major issue with using employment and destination as indicators of excellence and their subsequent importance is that there is a multiplicity of factors at play after the student leaves university, which the university has little influence on. For example, the university has little/no influence on the jobs that are

60 Struggle for a new reality

available; what processes are part of the application and interview procedure; and which jobs the individual will apply for. Yet, these factors are to be used to measure excellence.

The government at the time claimed that the three metrics critiqued above (NSS, retention and continuation, and graduate destination) have been developed '[a]fter informal discussions with the sector' (BIS, 2015, p. 33) though it was never made clear who had been involved in these. It is very concerning that the three metrics became six from 2017: Teaching on my course, Assessment and feedback, Academic support, Non-continuation, Employment or further study, highly skilled-employment or further study. The TEF is yet another device for marketability and commodification.

The succession of ministers since 2015 have been ambivalent about the possibility that metrics in the form of the TEF could be spurious instruments for measures of excellence, problematic and damaging to the purpose of universities, their academics, and the nature of learning. There was no evaluation of the impact of the metrics in the 2015 Green Paper (BIS, 2015) before going on to introduce new ones based on the presupposition of the effectiveness and appropriateness of metrics and the concept of excellence. Based on the critique that we have provided in this part of the book, we can foresee a time when TEF metrics, or something like them, will be included as part of the performance reviews of individual academics. It seems inevitable that questions about how individual academics contribute to the NSS and the retention/continuation and employment/destination metrics will become more explicitly a judgement of the performance of individuals and that this will be despite institutional/sectoral/structural limitations, such as resources. Currently, the TEF is used as part of recruitment/contract extensions, probation, and promotions; the final blow that will mark a significant moment for the neoliberalisation of the university and academics work will be when TEF-related benchmarks are actually linked to the pay of academics. Performance-related pay is already part of teaching contracts in schools and colleges, and if this becomes the case in HE then grade inflation will become an inevitability. The point here is that the 2015 Green Paper began a worrying trend that will traduce academics and their work, and the proposal for rolling out subject-level TEF, where individual academics will be identifiable for their contribution to ranking, needs to be actively and directly resisted if academics are to maintain their professional ethics and freedom. The stakes are high in every respect.

While it is abundantly clear that the TEF and NSS need to be abolished in the NES, the ongoing question that frames this and the way that academics ought to confront the performativity-based norm and reliance of spurious metrics are: how do we know what we do is effective? Effective for what purpose? What are the key issues to address problems? How do we celebrate successes? The nature of these questions is so subjective, that addressing them must be contextually specific. This means that academics in the NES should not be evaluated on external or national standardised benchmark measures. The success of the Finnish education system is based on the principles of professional autonomy and trust (Finnish National Board of Education, no date). In Engalnd, currently, there is a misleading autonomy associated with academics and the approach to their work. While there appears to be freedom to choose teaching methods, teaching materials, and student assessment mode and type, these are always contingent on external and structural factors associated with resources (ratio of staff to students etc.) and "what's best for the student" often means what will score well in league tables. Without the TEF and NSS, and part of the NES, academics must be trusted to be autonomous, without the toxifying effect of league tables. National league tables, especially those that are linked to national funding based on arbitrary targets, must be scrapped. Instead, league tables in the NES would be local to the university or a department, or a group of academics with similar aims and comparable objectives. The idea is that league tables can be localised and context-specific judgement of effectiveness but not used punitively. Trust would engender collectivity rather than oppositional competitiveness. DMU UCU (2019) proposed an alternative manifesto to the TEF and NSS, which is based on trust and collegiality. We have adapted their proposals, which we advocate as part of establishing principles and practices for the NES:

- Non-graded periodic self-led peer review of teaching. These are to celebrate success, development, and collegiality. The results would be locally managed and not for publication.
- A continuous cycle of workload review to include necessary allocation for reflection, maintenance of well-being, and of course research for teaching effectiveness. There should be nationally agreed allocations for duties, to protect workers and for transparency, in which trade unions play a role.
- Promotion should be equally available to all and based on merit judgements using criteria (not comparing individual academics). Promotion should be based on targets set by individuals as part of development meetings with line managers.

The DMU UCU (2019) also made a valuable suggestion about curriculum development, which as we have argued earlier, is increasingly being conditioned by a neoliberal agenda:

[T]he University should be built from the ground-up on co-operative principles, with teaching and learning based upon the students and staff working collectively to produce the curriculum. This should also be widened out to include the local community, ... [including] City Council and social/community organisations, and employers.

The NES presents an opportunity to reverse the damage caused by neoliberalism and reinstil ethics, professionalism, and integrity to academic life. Issues such as grade inflation, a crisis in academic/student identity, financialisation/marketisation of academic work could be resigned to the dustbin of history. Importantly, the relationship between competition and poor mental health will be broken with a new nature and purpose to higher education. Such has been the damage to the mental and psychological well-being of academics, arguably especially prospective academics and ECAs, that a genre of literature has emerged – *self-care* as a counter to the promotion of resilience. Earlier, we highlighted the tragic cases of Dr Anderson and Professor Canaan, the NES needs to focus on the way that the system impacts on the state of the individual generally. This has been the focus of O'Dwyer, Pinto, and McDonough's (2018) work, who highlight the importance of self-care of academics. They highlight the presence of metrics for all that is related to the academic's work (the number of publications, citations, student satisfaction) but none that accounts for the academic's general well-being. We follow O'Dwyer, Pinto, and McDonough (2018, p. 244) in suggesting, promotion of self-care as a priority in the NES, so that it becomes *systemic care*. By systemic care we mean an institutionalised promotion of individual and collective agency, which is about resisting those things that are seen as antithetical to the promotion of principles of the NES outlined earlier. As the opening epigram to this book pithily illustrates, currently academics feel alienated and voiceless in a system that disengages them (see also Hall, 2017, p. 11). Systemic care would not be about individuals being self-indulgent, it would be about their stake in the preservation of a new system that adheres to personal and professional politics and promotes HE as a collective public good (Lorde, 1988, in O'Dwyer, Pinto, and McDonough, p. 244).

In the previous chapter, we noted the emergence of Quit-Lit, which consists of a significant number of people who believe that universities and academic work have been too extensively and deeply neoliberalised to the point where they can no longer be salvaged. For them, the only feasible alternative available is to create alternative educational institutions away from the current neoliberal State.

Struggle for a new reality 63

Alternative universities

Drawing on work by Maisuria (in Maisuria and Cole, 2017) in this next section, we report a descriptive analysis of an example of alternative ways of organising a university, which is in stark contrast to and actively and openly subversive to the neoliberal model and its agenda. In the neoliberalised university, students are reduced to consumers, but a small group of people in Lincoln, England, began a project within the University of Lincoln in 2007 based on co-operative principles to recast students as "producers" of knowledge. Mike Neary and Gary Saunders as the founders described Student as Producer 'an act of collaboration between students and academics in the making of practical-critical knowledge' for change (Neary and Saunders, 2016, p. 9). The project was about critical and class consciousness for struggle as part of an educative experience. However, the project was within a neoliberal university, and this proved to be an impossible co-existence, thus providing a lesson about the way that neoliberalism makes difficult a decentring of neoliberal values. By 2011, Neary and Saunders (2016, p. 14) felt that the processes put in place to maintain the dissensual incorporation of Student as Producer into a mainstream institution 'appeared to have turned into just another bureaucratic management procedure'. Faced with what appeared to be a defeat, that year a group of staff from the University of Lincoln set up the Social Science Centre (Neary and Saunders, 2016, p. 15), which had no formal relationship with the university. In its own words (Social Science Centre, 2019), and drawing upon socialist and co-operative principles, the SSC stated its intentions:

> Social Science Centre offers opportunities to engage in a co-operative experience of higher education. Run as a not-for-profit co-operative, the SSC is organised on the basis of democratic, non-hierarchical principles, with all members having equal involvement in the life and work of the SSC. Staff and students are at the centre study themes that draw on the core subjects in social science: sociology, politics and philosophy, as well as psychology, economics, journalism and photography. The Centre organises study and research at all levels including undergraduate, Masters and Doctorates in Philosophy.
>
> The co-operative principles that guide the organisation of the SSC also extend to the ways in which they design and run their courses. All classes are participative and collaborative in order to ground inquiry in the experiences and knowledges of the participants. Student-scholars and teacher-scholars have opportunities to design courses together, and those new to teaching and independent learning are offered generous support from others. All members are able to work with

academics and other experienced researchers on research projects, and to publish their own writings through the SSC. One key guiding principle of the Centre is that 'teachers' and 'students' have much to learn from each other.

The "Student as Producer" model of learning and teaching was the heartbeat of the enterprise. As Neary and Saunders (2016, p. 2) put it:

'Student as Producer' is an act of resistance to the current policy framework being imposed on universities in England and around the world and, as such, is a critical response to attempts by national governments to create and consolidate a consumerist culture and impose high levels of debt among undergraduate students.

'Student as Producer', they continue, 'emerged from this double crisis: a socio-economic crisis and an associated crisis over the meaning and purpose of higher education', and 'identifies strongly with the academic and student movement of protests against fees and cuts to funding in higher education and other social and welfare services' (Neary and Saunders, 2016, p. 2).

Countering the commodification and marketisation of degrees, Student as Producer – taking its title from Walter Benjamin's The Author as Producer, in which he argues that not only should intellectual authors produce revolutionary publications, they should also seek to transform the social relations of production for a communist society – 'is framed around the practices and principles of critical pedagogy, popular education and Marxist theory'. With respect to Marxist theory, in addition to the inspiration coming from Benjamin, Neary and Saunders (2016, p. 2) refer to Thomas Mathiesen's notion of the 'politics of abolition' and his underpinning concept of 'the unfinished' (Mathiesen, 1974, cited in Neary and Saunders, 2016, p. 3). This relates to the Gramscian idea that dominant hegemony is never hermetically sealed, which is based upon the Marx's proposition that history is open to new and different ways of unfolding, and continuous struggle and solidarity is what changes the world.

In this way, the establishment of the SSC was itself an act of negation, and the role and function of it was to contribute to social transformation through revolutionary knowledge building: 'revolutionary knowledge is understood as something that is constituted through class struggle, co-operation and radical practice, where the crisis of the capitalist university becomes a field of radical research to be reconstituted as a form of subversive "living knowledge"' (Roggero, 2011, p. 8, cited in Neary and Saunders, 2016, p. 3).

Struggle for a new reality 65

The SSC practised what has been called critical pedagogy, revolutionary critical pedagogy, popular education, and public pedagogy. One of the architects of contemporary critical pedagogy is Peter McLaren, who provides the foreword to this book. For McLaren (2015, p. 27), critical pedagogy

> locates the production of critical knowledges leading to praxis in its social, spatial and geopolitical contexts, and reveals the workings of the production process and how it operates intertextually alongside and upon other discourses, but it does so with a particular political project in mind – an anti-capitalist, anti-imperialist, anti-racist, anti-sexist and pro-democratic and emancipatory struggle.

Earlier, we have noted that the curriculum is being increasingly colonised by market forces and commercial demands, and that it has become increasingly difficult to do critical and creative work, particularly that which targets structural and political neoliberalism. Critical pedagogy is suggested as an antidote by McLaren (see for example McLaren, 2015, pp. 27–28) who states that critical pedagogy has the potential to work against power relations, by exposing them and articulating them with neoliberalism, in the way that we have described as reflective criticality earlier in this book. Important to critical pedagogy, which we suggest underpins the learning and teaching in any alternative university, is developing "popular education". Popular education is a nod towards connecting university/academic work with a consideration of how wider public and individual benefits can be derived through resistance and an alternative to become feasible in consciousness and in practice. This is different from the personal investment that is central to the neoliberal university.

In the context of critical pedagogy, popular education, and Student as Producer, the SSC could be situated in Marx's early writings because students are required to recognise themselves as having the agentive capacity to create their own learning with others (Neary and Saunders, 2016, p. 11), which is antithetical to the neoliberal model. An important feature of the SSC model of education was that the curriculum was co-constructed. Hanson (2017, p. 242) explains:

> A key aspect ... is that the 'teaching' sessions are co-produced: we build knowledge through the discussion of texts rather than having an academic coming in to tell you things; although there are academics who know a lot of things at SSC, and everyone involved has access to them. The hard student-teacher dichotomy has been lost. There are members and scholars, members run things to whatever extent

66 *Struggle for a new reality*

they wish to, and scholars come in and engage with what we do for free, but there isn't much of a barrier between the two.

The SSC showed that the re-imagining of teaching and learning to be a collaborative, exploratory, and solidaristic activity is feasible, rather than built on a financial transaction extinguishing the process of learning and focusing on the purchase – a commodity. This must be part of a new education structure and ethos, and central to the NES. The explication here is that financialisation poisons the whole nature of learning and teaching. The proposal of the NES includes the abolition of tuition fees. Fees in England are the highest in the world, even higher than the US where accommodation is included in the price and many students can access bursaries, sponsorships, and fee waivers. There will be significant opposition to making higher education free. Much of this opposition will be financial but also cultural in nature, and the main question would be, where will the money come from? The estimated cost of making HE free in England is between £8 and £12 billion, which is very cheap considering the social and economic returns. For every pound that is *invested* into public services, the productivity returns off-set the cost; the principle here is the same as the one neoliberals use about incurring personal debt for individualised prosperity. In terms of social returns, Pickett and Wilkinson in their books *Spirit Level* and *The Inner level* convincingly show that the more marketised and individualised society is, the worse off everybody in that society will be (The Equality Trust, 2019). They show that there will be more health and social problems, particularly physical health, mental health, drug abuse, education, imprisonment, obesity, social mobility, trust and community life, violence, teenage pregnancies, and child well-being; outcomes are significantly worse in more unequal rich countries (see The Equality Trust, 2019). Having a tuition-free university sector will lead to more effective learning and improve the society for everyone. It just needs the political will to create a fairer taxation system meaning progressive and higher taxation, where the NES would be disproportionately funded by the richest individuals and corporations through, for example, income and wealth taxes.

The meta principle at play here is the redistribution of wealth for the public good. Neoliberalism has been such a powerful force for cultural production that impinges on consciousness, that people find it difficult to countenance free education. The SSC had been successfully offering exactly this in Lincoln, and such was the success of this as an alternative with a need for expanding, that Steve Hanson created a second SSC in Manchester:

> It was very important to those involved in Manchester that we start another branch of SSC, rather than create our own idiosyncratic, egotistical

[free university] project: SSC is also about movement-building, long term, about providing free access and appropriate 'quality' for the humanities.

(Hanson, 2017, p. 243)

Hanson goes on to make clear that the SSC was about changing the nature of what higher education could be:

Marketisation is not just about money and access. The very fabric of mainstream universities is being warped significantly by their changing structures. We may have to consider a different name to 'university' in some cases. This is how 'quality' signifies here.

(ibid.)

This neoliberal nature and fabric must be changed, but the fate of the SSC shows that it is a struggle. The founders of the original SSC, Neary and Saunders (2016), stressed that despite creating the Student as Producer model of education, they were still in existence in the neoliberal world – there is no outside of it; the SSC was *in and against* the neoliberal system.

Working against the dominant hegemony of neoliberalism to create the SSC was a momentous task, and for seven years it did what it set out to do, but neoliberalism is aggressive and efficacious in maintaining its own dominant hegemony and the SSC was forced to fold and closed off with this farewell statement on the home page (Social Science Centre, 2019):

[O]rganised and run free, co-operative higher education courses and community projects in the city of Lincoln. The SSC was created as both a critique of and an alternative to the dominant model of higher education in the UK, and has been inspirational for many of its members and followers. It has created many spaces for intellectual life, learning, solidarity and friendship within the city and enabled many of us to follow new dreams. Running such a project has required considerable time and commitment from us all, and [has] been challenging at times, and we have reached the limit of what we are able to achieve in this organisational form.

The SSC was the second alternative free provider to succumb, the first being the Free University of Liverpool (FUL) which closed after three years in 2013. It is plausible to ask where does this leave us? It is quite clear that countenancing the possibility and material reality of an alternative being feasible, and also exposing difficulties associated, are the greatest contribution that the SSC made. Part of this learning from history is that the neoliberal higher education landscape is evolving with marketisation deepening. This has led Hanson (2017) to question whether alternative providers will need to consider expanding into the mainstream to stay financially viable, and if so, what are the consequences? Can the underpinning principles be maintained? Hanson (2017, pp. 254–255) states the critical importance of policy introduction circa 2015/2016, meaning that students are now legally reframed as consumers and customers enshrined as part of the Higher Education and Research Act 2017, which brings universities within the jurisdiction of the Competition & Markets Authority (CMA) and the Consumer Rights Act (CRA) (Higher Education and Research Act, 2017). The 'buyer-seller logic' (Hanson, 2017, p. 257) that has been creeping in is now firmly established, and a practical question that Hanson raises is whether this language would need to be adopted by alternative providers. This could mean an inherent comprise of co-operative principles, and as such 'Student and teacher now fully face each other on either side of a binarial division of labour that is framed antagonistically rather than co-productively' (ibid. p. 258). Similarly, these co-operative principles may be difficult or impossible to exist in regulatory and metrics-based assessment frameworks under the guise of quality/excellence and value for money. Hanson (ibid., p. 262) summarises the consequence in the following terms, 'there is a HE culture almost monomaniacally focused on risk management in the face of potential litigation. These risks are not hallucinatory; they are encouraged and enabled by the structures that are meant to be warding them off'.

There is no precedent for an alternative university to exist within the neoliberal mainstream, but it does exist resonating most closely with the alternative child-centred independent school – Summerhill, which has had a turbulent relationship with the inspectorate Ofsted. Ofsted has regularly asked the school to be more closely governed with tighter managerial practices and to have a closer adherence to national frameworks on standards, both of which reduce the co-construction and autonomy elements of progressive child-centred pedagogy (see Ofsted, 2019; Summerhill, no date).

The SSC has been an experiment to test the sustainability of an alternative plurally existing along side mainstream neoliberal universities. Perhaps the most significant experience to draw on from the SSC for strategic thinking about future planning is the issue of financialisation. It seems that the SSC and LFU were both able to withstand cultural pressures, i.e. recognition and legitimacy, but the financial burden, without fees in a system that relies on money, was too great. Since the SSC met its "limit", the Co-operative University in Manchester is set to exploit the opportunity afforded in the HE Bill of 2017. It will be an institution that will integrate into the structures of mainstream universities, effectively expanding choice in the HE market. The proposal is to open in 2019/2020 with four courses and ambitiously,

Struggle for a new reality   69

the university will also accredit co-operative partners (Co-operative University, 2019).

The most important aspect of all this is the introduction of a fee of £5,500 per annum based upon part-time study over a total of four years (Co-operative University, 2019). The introduction of the fees will be another test, especially: in what ways can it still be regarded as an alternative to neoliberal universities? How will the ethos achieve the CMA and other neoliberal targets? If the rest of the providers in the market eventually drop their fees to £7500 as widely expected, how will this impact?

The creation of the Co-operative University appears to be enacting many of the principles of democracy, participation, and representation that are being fought for by the DMU UCU discussed earlier. These appear to be explained as part of five statements about what makes the Co-operative University unique (Co-operative University, 2019): They were constructed through input from: co-operators, potential students, academics, teachers, researchers, colleagues, and general enthusiasts.

Here they are, in no particular order:

Not afraid of the big issues: A Co-operative University has a responsibility to tackle the big issues of our time, with a commitment to supporting social change and reinvigorating radical ideas. The Co-operative University will explore a whole range of issues, from the world of work (and how we do this, equitably, in the future) to how we take a values-based approach to looking after the planet and our neighbourhoods as citizens.

Developing the skills needed to identify, understand, and make positive change will be a big part of participating in the Co-operative University. Running courses which have content focused on the role of co-operation in forging a better social, economic, and political world cannot be negotiable!

How we'll be governed: A second difference prioritised by Information Day participants was the importance of co-operative governance. Although it is the Co-operative College that is formally seeking Degree Awarding Powers on behalf of the federation of Higher Education Co-operatives, a Co-operative University will be wholeheartedly co-operative in the way that it is governed.

You want a one member one vote system and for students, academics, and all support staff to be members. So do we. Sound democratic practice is critical to everything we do. As the federation grows, there will be a need to continuously reflect on and test what is working and what isn't, but a university with a vibrant co-operative model of governance is one of our 'red lines'.

It's arguably the main difference between the traditional university and the Co-operative one and we know from many of the responses that we've received that it's important to you too.

Agility: A third difference is the innovative nature of the Co-operative University model and the impact this could have in terms of disrupting the status quo. The new university may not be huge (compared to lots of other universities), but there will be significant advantages in keeping to a manageable scale. A Co-operative University will offer an alternative model to other education institutions globally, showing how things can be done differently.

Absence of hierarchy: Reason number four focuses on a lack of hierarchy and a commitment to inclusivity. This will set the Co-operative University apart from the traditional or neoliberal model. This lack of hierarchy is characterised by our governance model too, as explained above. We want to foster a shared responsibility amongst everyone involved for making this university work, and that's what we're committed to doing.

An extraordinary academic experience: Last but not least, the final major difference between a Co-operative University and its traditional counterparts will be the way in which the teaching, learning, and research take place. Our research told us that you wanted to see significant student input into the content and design of courses and in how students do their learning. You believe that the knowledge produced in a Co-operative University will be different because it will have been created in a strongly collaborative, values-driven, and co-operative way. We agree and can't wait to build an extraordinary academic experience together.

Clearly and perhaps inevitably, finances emerged as a major problem for the SSC and LFU, the Co-operative University may off-set this fatalistic danger by succumbing to fees and being more integrated in the mainstream neoliberal market of universities. While the principle of a free education seems to have changed into *more affordable* with £5,500 rather than £9,250 fees, the commitments above seem to suggest a desire to maintain the core commitment of creative and critical thinking, combined with autonomy and freedom, and democracy – all with the purpose of using education for the greater good.

What will come of it will be important to address the question of what kind of alternative higher education may exist in neoliberalism, and against neoliberalism. However, we want to reframe this question by suggesting that an NES provides an alternative to the alternative. The Quit-Lit scholars all commonly state the impossibility of working with different (socialist/solidaristic)

Struggle for a new reality 71

principles within a neoliberal state, which we agree with. However, in this book we have laid out a broad argument for the creation of an NES, which would have at its core the co-operative principles, such as free education, *and* be within a State system of higher education. In the NES, the universities sector can be envisioned as consisting of nationwide institutions that are autonomous, having localised accountability, with the State responsible for upholding the principles of autonomy, freedom, and the promotion of the public good. There would be no problem about the suffocating nature of a highly centralised system, and a report compiled by a team of independent experts for the Labour Party demonstrates the feasibility of achieving this (see Barrott et al., 2017). There would be no private universities, minimal competition linked to financial sustainability, and marketisation would be part of progressing human flourishing, not an individual's earning capacity. Academic workers and universities have lost too much ground to neoliberalism, it means there is a lot to gain. Giroux (2016) puts this pithily: 'We don't need tepid calls for repairing the system; instead, we need to invent a new system from the ashes of one that is terminally broken'. The vision for/of the NES will not overcome neoliberalism instantaneously but it will create a significant space to do critical work against neoliberalism that could build the potential and impetus for sociocultural and political-economic revolutionary change. Given the slide towards an American style education system as described by Peter McLaren in the foreword to this book and also by Henry Giroux (2014), there is everything to fight for. This is the provocation we leave you with.

Note

1 This section updates Alpesh Maisuria's contribution to Maisuria and Cole (2017, pp. 8–10).

References

Acker, S., Webber, M. (2017) 'Made to measure: Early career academics in the Canadian university workplace', *Higher Education Research & Development*, 36(3), pp. 541–554.

Ainley, P., Allen, M. (2010) *Lost Generation?: New Strategies for Youth and Education*. London, UK: Continuum.

Allen, M., Ainley, P. (2007) *Education Make You Fick, Innit?* London, UK: Tufnell Press.

Allen, M. (2019) 'Can you ever be "overeducated"?', *Education, economy, and society*, 6 May. Available at: https://education-economy-society.com/2019/05/06/can-you-ever-be-overeducated/?fbclid=IwAR0Ee1k35cX35yLA-WKI53rNkfGJy-6f0RyK-Iy9GH2ApsGY4W2n86L4bJBQ#comment-15055 (Accessed: 22 May 2019).

Adams, J. (2017) *We need to rethink research funding for UK regions to prosper*. Available at: www.theguardian.com/higher-education-network/2017/jun/05/rethink-research-funding-uk-regions-prosper (Accessed: 26 August 2018).

Amsler, S. (2010) *The death of philosophy in the neoliberal world*. Available at: http://isa-universities-in-crisis.isa-sociology.org/?p=464 (Accessed: 28 August 2018).

Amsler, S. (2011) 'Beyond all reason: Spaces of hope in the struggle for England's universities', *Representations*, 116(1), pp. 62–87.

Amsler, S., Bolsmann, C. (2012) 'University ranking as social exclusion', *British Journal of Sociology of Education*, 33(2), pp. 283–301.

Anonymous Academic (2015) *My students have paid £9,000 and now they think they own me*. Available at: www.theguardian.com/higher-education-network/2015/dec/18/my-students-have-paid-9000-and-now-they-think-they-own-me (Accessed: 27 August 2018).

Anonymous Academic (2018a) *My students support our strike – they don't want to be passive consumers*. Available at: www.theguardian.com/higher-education-network/2018/mar/02/my-students-support-our-strike-they-dont-want-to-be-passive-consumers (Accessed: 20 August 2018).

Anonymous Academic (2018b) *Teaching off-the-shelf curricula does university students a disservice*. Available at: www.theguardian.com/higher-education-network/2018/jun/08/teaching-off-the-shelf-curricula-does-university-students-a-disservice (Accessed: 20 August 2018).

References

Anonymous Academic (2019) *My university accepts overseas students who are doomed to fail*. Available at: www.theguardian.com/education/2019/feb/08/my-university-accepts-overseas-students-who-are-doomed-to-fail (Accessed: 20 June 2019).

Astarita, C. (2018) 'Karl Marx and the transition from feudalism to capitalism', *International Critical Thought*, 8(2), pp. 249–263.

Baggini, J. (2018) 'If universities sacrifice philosophy on the altar of profit, what's next?', *The Guardian*. 21 December. Available at: www.theguardian.com/commentisfree/2018/dec/21/universities-philosophy-profit-business-partners

Ball, S.J. (2000) 'Performativities and fabrications in the education economy: Towards the performative society', *Australian Educational Researcher*, 17(3), pp. 1–24.

Ball, S.J. (2003) 'The teacher's soul and the terrors of performativity', *Journal of Education Policy*, 18(2), pp. 215–228.

Ball, S.J. (2012) *Global Education Inc.: New Policy Networks and the Neoliberal Imaginary*. Oxon, UK: Routledge.

Ball, S.J. (2017) *The Education Debate*, 3rd ed. Bristol, UK: Policy Press.

Banfield, G., Maisuria, A., Raduntz, H. (2016) 'The (Im)possibility of the intellectual worker inside the neoliberal university', *Educação & Formação [Journal of Education & Training]*, 1(3), pp. 3–19.

Barrott, C., Brown, M., Cumbers, A., Hope, C., Huckfield, L., Calvert Jump, R., McInroy, N., Shaw, L. (2017) *Alternative models of ownership*. Available at: https://labour.org.uk/wp-content/uploads/2017/10/Alternative-Models-of-Ownership.pdf (Accessed: 22 April 2019).

BBC News (2019) *Lecturer's widow hits out at Cardiff University workload*. Available at: www.bbc.co.uk/news/uk-wales-47296631 (Accessed: 22 April 2019).

Becker, G. (1964) *Human Capital: A Theoretical and Empirical Analysis with Special Reference to Education*. Chicago, IL: University of Chicago Press.

Beckmann, A., Cooper, C., Hill, D. (2009) 'Neoliberalization and managerialization of 'education' in England and Wales – a case for reconstructing education', *Journal for Critical Education Policy Studies*, 7(2), pp. 310–345.

Bell, D. (1973) *The Coming of Post-Industrial Society: A Venture in Social Forecasting*. New York, NY: Basic Books.

Bellamy Foster, J., Yates, M.D. (2014) 'Piketty and the crisis of neoclassical economics', *Monthly Review – An Independent Socialist Magazine*, 66(6), pp. 1–24.

BIS (2015) *Fulfilling our potential: Teaching excellence, social mobility and student choice*. Available at: www.timeshighereducation.com/sites/default/files/breaking_news_files/green_paper.pdf (Accessed: 27 August 2018).

Black, P., Wiliam, D. (1998) 'Inside the black box: Raising standards through classroom assessment', *Phi Delta Kappa International*, 80(2), pp. 139–144, 146–148.

Bolton, P. (2017) *Tuition fee statistics*. London, UK: House of Commons Library. Available at: http://researchbriefings.files.parliament.uk/documents/SN00917/SN00917.pdf (Accessed: 2 August 2018).

References

Boronski, T., Hassan, N. (2015) *Sociology of Education*. London, UK: Sage.
Boulter, C. (2011) *Performativity*. Available at: https://youtu.be/t-mM-7ly9Jo (Accessed: 17 August 2018).
Bowles, S., Gintis, H. (1976) *Schooling in Capitalist America: Educational Reform and the Contradictions of Economic Life*. London, UK: Routledge & Kegan Paul Ltd.
Bowring, F. (2004) 'From the mass worker to the multitude: A theoretical contextualisation of Hardt and Negri's Empire', *Capital & Class*, 83, pp. 101–132.
Bristow, A., Robinson, S., Ratle, O. (2017) 'Being and early-career CMS academic in the context of insecurity and 'Excellence': The dialectics of resistance and compliance', *Organization Studies*, 38(9), pp. 1185–1207.
Busby, E. (2018) *University strikes: Students set to receive 'direct compensation' over lectures missed due to action, minister says*. Available at: www.independent.co.uk/news/education/education-news/university-strikes-compensation-lecturers-students-sam-gyimah-direct-minister-latest-a8232746.html (Accessed: 20 August 2018).
Canaan, J., Shumar, W. (2008) *Structure and Agency in the Neoliberal University*. New York, NY: Routledge.
Canaan, J. (2013) 'Resisting the English neoliberalising university: What critical pedagogy can offer', *Journal for Critical Education Studies*, 11(2), pp. 16–56.
Canaan, J. (2016) *Conversation to Alpesh Maisuria*, 03 March.
Carey, K. (2019) 'The creeping capitalist takeover of higher education', *Huffington Post*. 1 April. Available at: www.huffpost.com/highline/article/capitalist-takeover-college/
Cleaver, H. (1992) 'The inversion of class perspective in Marxian theory: From valorisation to self-valorisation', in Bonefeld, W. Gunn, R. & Psychopedis, K. (eds.) *Open Marxism Volume II: Theory and Practice*, pp. 106–144. London, UK: Pluto.
Cruickshank, J. (2016) 'Putting business at the heart of higher education: On neoliberal interventionism and audit culture in UK universities', *Open Library of Humanities*, 2(1), pp. 1–33.
Collini, S. (2018) 'In UK universities there is a daily erosion of integrity', *The Guardian*. Available at: www.theguardian.com/education/2018/apr/24/uk-universities-erosion-integrity-bologna-statement
Co-operative University (2019) *What makes us different*. Available at: www.co-op.ac.uk/Pages/Category/co-operative-university (Accessed: 2 June 2019).
Coventry Observer (2018) *City MP submits parliamentary motion to debate Coventry University union dispute*. Available at: https://coventryobserver.co.uk/news/city-mp-submits-parliamentary-motion-to-debate-coventry-university-union-dispute/?fbclid=IwAR1ev-UW-x37odb7KIxAxOO5skH2y_I4F0diu3L-6JsMDEclBHriSj9ivV1E (Accessed: 2 June 2019).
Davies, B., Bansel, P. (2007) 'Neoliberalism and education', *International Journal of Qualitative Studies in Education*, 20(3), pp. 247–259.
Davies, W. (2014) *The Limits of Neoliberalism: Authority, Sovereignty and the Logic of Competition*. London, UK: SAGE.

76 References

Dehaye, P.O. (2016) 'MOOC platforms, surveillance, and control', *Academe*, 102(5), pp. 31–33.

Department for Education (2018) *Graduate labour market statistics 2017.* Available at: https://assets.publishing.service.gov.uk/government/uploads/system/uploads/attachment_data/file/701720/GLMS_2017.pdf (Accessed: 26 August 2018).

Department of Business Innovation and Skills (2009) *Higher ambitions: The future of universities in a knowledge economy – executive summary.* Available at: http://webarchive.nationalarchives.gov.uk/+/http:/www.bis.gov.uk/wp-content/uploads/publications/Higher-Ambitions.pdf (Accessed: 26 June 2018).

Department of Business Innovation and Skills (2016) *Success as a knowledge economy: Teaching excellence, social mobility and student choice.* Available at: https://assets.publishing.service.gov.uk/government/uploads/system/uploads/attachment_data/file/523396/bis-16-265-success-as-a-knowledge-economy.pdf (Accessed: 3 July 2018).

Department for Education and Sam Gyimah MP (2018) *Speech: A revolution in accountability.* Available at: www.gov.uk/government/speeches/a-revolution-in-accountability (Accessed: 26 August 2018).

DMU UCU (2019) *DMU renewed. A manifesto.* Available at: https://ucudemontfort.wordpress.com/2019/02/11/dmu-renewed-a-manifesto-for-change/ (Accessed: 3 June 2019).

Dobinson, I. (2018) *Royal holloway 'suspends' the university union's equalities and diversity officer.* Available at: www.getsurrey.co.uk/news/surrey-news/royal-holloway-suspends-university-unions-14630195 (Accessed: 28 August 2018).

Doward, J., Bennett, G. (2018) *Defence contractors hand British universities £40m.* Available at: www.theguardian.com/world/2018/mar/31/defence-contractors-british-universities-funding (Accessed: 20 August 2018).

Donoghue, F. (2008) *The Last Professors: The Corporate University and the Fate of the Humanities.* New York, NY: Fordham University Press.

Drucker, P.F. (1969) *The Age of Discontinuity: Guidelines to Our Changing Society.* London, UK: Heinemann.

Eddy, P.L., Gaston-Gayles, J.L. (2008) 'New faculty on the block: Issues of stress and support', *Journal of Human Behavior in the Social Environment*, 17(1–2), pp. 89–106.

Engels, F. (2009) *The Condition of the Working Class in England.* London, UK: Penguin.

Evans, G. (2018) *Struggling universities will be shut down, not saved – it's not fair for students.* Available at: www.theguardian.com/higher-education-network/2018/feb/05/struggling-universities-will-be-shut-down-not-saved-its-not-fair-for-students (Accessed: 26 August 2018).

Fazackerley, A. (2018) *Fears of university closure after removal of safety net.* Available at: www.theguardian.com/education/2018/jan/30/fears-university-closures-office-for-students (Accessed: 26 August 2018).

References

Fazackerley, A. (2019) *'It's cut-throat': Half of UK academics stressed and 40% thinking of leaving*. Available at: www.theguardian.com/education/2019/may/21/cut-throat-half-academics-stressed-thinking-leaving (Accessed: 18 June 2019).

Finnish National Board of Education (no date) *Teachers in Finland – trusted professionals*. Available at: www.oph.fi/download/148960_Teachers_in_Finland.pdf (Accessed: 18 June 2019).

Fisher, G. (2007) '"You need tits to get on round here": Gender and sexuality in the entrepreneurial university of the 21st century', *Ethnography*, 8, pp. 503–517.

Fisher, M. (2009) *Capitalist Realism: Is There No Alternative?* Hants, UK: o-books.

Fitzner, J. (2017) 'Neoliberalism and illusion: The importance of preparing students to live in the 21st century', *Journal for Critical Education Policy Studies*, 15(2), pp. 214–239.

Ford, D.R. (2017) 'Studying like a communist: Affect, the party, and the educational limits to capitalism', *Educational Philosophy and Theory*, 49(5), pp. 452–461.

Freire, P. (January 1985) 'Reading the world and reading the word: An interview with Paulo Freire', *Language Arts*, 62(1), pp. 15–21.

Forgacs, D. (2000) *The Gramsci Reader: Selected Writings 1916–1935*. New York: New York University Press.

Fulcher, J. (2015) *Capitalism: A Very Short Introduction*. Oxford, UK: Oxford University Press.

Furedi, F. (June 2009) 'Now is the age of the discontented', *Times Higher Education*, 4–10(1,899), pp. 30–35.

Fyles, F.S. (2018) *Universities withholding millions from staff involved in UCU strike*. Available at: http://felixonline.co.uk/articles/2018-06-07-universities-withholding-millions-from-staff-involved-in-ucu-strike/ (Accessed: 20 August 2018).

Gardner, B. (2014) *Professor suspended from top university for giving off 'negative vibes'*. Available at: www.telegraph.co.uk/education/11187063/Professor-suspended-from-top-university-for-giving-off-negative-vibes.html (Accessed: 28 August 2018).

Geoghegan, P. (2018) 13 July. Available at: https://twitter.com/peterkgeoghegan/status/1017697090619826176?lang=en (Accessed: 28 August 2018).

Gee, A. (2017) *Facing poverty, adjuncts turn to sex work and sleeping in cars*. Available at: www.theguardian.com/us-news/2017/sep/28/adjunct-professors-homeless-sex-work-academia-poverty (Accessed: 12 June 2019).

Gill, J. (2017) *Teachers like the work but not the workplace*. Available at: www.timeshighereducation.com/comment/teachers-work-not-workplace (Accessed: 27 August 2018).

Gill, R., Pratt, A. (2008) 'In the social factory? Immaterial labour, precariousness and cultural work', *Theory, Culture & Society*, 25(7–8), pp. 1–30.

Gillies, D. (2011) 'State education as high-yield investment: Human capital theory in European policy discourse', *Journal of Pedagogy*, 2(2), pp. 224–245.

Giroux, H.A. (2003) 'Selling out higher education', *Policy Futures in Education*, 1, pp. 179–200.

References

Giroux, H.A. (2014) *Neoliberalism's War on Higher Education*. London, UK: Haymarket Books.

Giroux, H.A. (2016) *Radical politics in the age of American authoritarianism: Connecting the dots*. Available at: https://truthout.org/articles/radical-politics-in-the-age-of-american-authoritarianism-connecting-the-dots/ (Accessed: 10 June 2019).

Gorlewski, J. (2016) '"Say what they want to hear": Students' perceptions of writing in a working class high school', *Journal for Critical Education Policy Studies*, 14(2), pp. 158–185.

Gramsci, A. (1971) *Selections from the Prison Notebooks*. Hoare, Q. and Smith, G.N. London, UK: Lawrence & Wishart.

Green, A. (2007) *Conversation to Alpesh Maisuria*, 03 March.

Green, F., Kynaston, D. (2019) 'The 7 per cent problem: How to reform private schools', *New Statesman*. Available at: www.newstatesman.com/politics/education/2019/06/7-cent-problem-how-reform-private-schools (Accessed: 10 June 2019).

Hall, R. (2013) 'Educational technology and the enclosure of academic labour inside public higher education', *Journal for Critical Education Policy Studies*, 11(3), pp. 52–82.

Hall, R. (2015a) 'The university and the secular crisis', *Open Library of Humanities*, 1(1), pp. 1–33.

Hall, R. (2015b) 'The implication of autonomist Marxism for research and practice in education and technology', *Learning, Media and Technology*, 40(1), pp. 106–122.

Hall, R. (2015c) 'For a political economy of massive open online courses', *Learning, Media and Technology*, online first.

Hall, R. (2017) *On the alienation of academic labour and the possibilities for mass intellectuality*. Available at: www.dora.dmu.ac.uk/xmlui/handle/2086/14300 (Accessed: 28 March 2018).

Hall, R., Smyth, K. (2016) 'Dismantling the curriculum in higher education', *Open Library of Humanities*, 2(1), pp. 1–27.

Hall, R. (2019) *Are PhDs just cheap labour for universities?* Available at: www.theguardian.com/education/2019/apr/01/are-phds-just-cheap-labour-for-universities (Accessed: 27 May 2019).

Hanson, S. (2017) 'Language, juridical epistemologies and power in the new UK university: Can alternative providers escape?', *Journal for Critical Education Policy Studies*, 15(3), pp. 241–265.

Harvey, D. (2007) *A Brief History of Neoliberalism*. Oxford, UK: Oxford University Press.

Hatcher, R. (2001) 'Getting down to the business: Schooling in the globalised economy', *Education and Social Justice*, 3(2), pp. 45–59.

Hatcher, T. (2013) 'Robert Owen: A historiographic study of a pioneer of human resource development', *European Journal of Training and Development*, 37(4), pp. 414–431.

Higher Education and Research Act (2017) Available at: www.legislation.gov.uk/ukpga/2017/29/pdfs/ukpga_20170029_en.pdf (Accessed: 28 August 2018).

References

Hill, D. (2004) 'Global capital, neo-liberalism, and privatization: The growth of educational inequality', in Hill, D., Cole, M. (eds.) *Schooling and Equality: Fact, Concept and Policy*, pp. 35–54. Oxon, UK: RoutledgeFalmer.

Hill, D. (2013) *Marxist Essays on Neoliberalism, Class, 'Race', Capitalism and Education*. Brighton, UK: The Institute for Education Policy Studies.

Hill, D., Kumar, R. (2009) *Global Neoliberalism and Education and its Consequences*. London, UK: Routledge.

Hill, D., Lewis, C., Maisuria, A., Yarker, P., Carr, J. (2015) Neoliberal and neoconservative immiseration capitalism in England: Policies and impacts on society and on education. *Journal for Critical Education Policy Studies. The Institute for Education Policy Studies*. 13(2), 38–82.

Hillman, N. (2018) *Ministers are anything but relaxed about university closures*. Available at: www.timeshighereducation.com/opinion/ministers-are-anything-relaxed-about-university-closures (Accessed: 26 August 2018).

Institute for Fiscal Studies (2017) *Higher education funding in England: Past, present and options for the future*. Available at: www.ifs.org.uk/uploads/publications/bns/BN211.pdf (Accessed: 26 August 2018).

Institute for Fiscal Studies (2018) *The relative labour market returns to different degrees*. Available at: https://assets.publishing.service.gov.uk/government/uploads/system/uploads/attachment_data/file/714517/The_relative_labour_market-returns_to_different_degrees.pdf (Accessed: 26 August 2018).

Isomöttönen, V. (2018) 'For the oppressed teacher: stay real!', *Teaching in Higher Education*, 23(7), pp. 869–884.

Jaeger, E.L. (2017) 'Reproducing vulnerability: A Bourdieuian analysis or readers who struggle in neoliberal times', *British Journal of Sociology of Education*, 38(7), pp. 975–990.

Jones, C. (2017) *Bane of the postgrad lecturer – teaching students your own age*. Available at: www.theguardian.com/education/2017/jun/22/postgraduates-who-teach-how-to-lecture-undergraduates (Accessed: 28 August 2018).

Kallio, K., Kallio, T.J., Grossi, G. (2017) 'Performance measurement in universities: Ambiguities in the use of quality versus quantity in performance indicators', *Public Money & Management*, 37(4), pp. 293–300.

Koukal, D.R. (2010) 'All that is solid melts into air', *Technology and Culture*, 51(1), pp. 227–231.

Kriedte, P., Medick, H., Schlumbohm, J. (1981) *Industrialization before Industrialization: Rural Industry in the Genesis of Capitalism*. Cambridge, UK: Cambridge University Press.

Labour Party (2017) *Manifesto*. Available at: https://labour.org.uk/manifesto/ (Accessed: 15 June 2019).

Lauder, H., Young, M., Daniels, H., Balarin, M., Lowe, J. (2012) *Educating for the Knowledge Economy? Critical Perspectives*. Oxon, UK: Routledge.

Leathwood, C., Read, B. (2013) 'Research policy and academic performativity: Compliance, contestation and complicity', *Studies in Higher Education*, 38(8), pp. 1162–1174.

Lippit, V.D. (2005) *Capitalism*. Oxon, UK: Routledge.

References

Livingstone, D.W., Scholtz, A. (2016) 'Reconnecting class and production relations in an advanced capitalist 'knowledge economy': Changing class structure and class consciousness', *Capital & Class*, 40(3), pp. 469–493.

Loick, D. (2018) 'If you're a critical theorist, how come you work for a university?', *Critical Horizons*, 19(3), pp. 233–245.

London School of Economics and Political Science (2018) *Graduate destinations.* Available at: www.lse.ac.uk/International-History/Degrees/graduate-destinations (Accessed: 27 August 2018).

Lynch, R., Baines, P. (2004) 'Strategy development in UK higher education: Towards resource-based competitive advantages', *Journal of Higher Education Policy and Management*, 26(2), pp. 171–187.

Macfarlane, B. (2016) 'Collegiality and performativity in a competitive academic culture', *Higher Education Review*, 48(2), pp. 31–50.

Macfarlane, B. (December 2018) The CV as a symbol of the changing nature of academic life: Performativity, prestige and self-presentation. *Studies in Higher Education.* doi: 10.1080/03075079.2018.1554638.

Maisuria, A. (2011) 'Ten years of new labour education policy and radical inequality: An act of whiteness or neo-liberal practice?', in Green, T. (ed.) *Blair's Educational Legacy and Prospects: Then Years of New Labour*, pp. 171–191. London, UK: Palgrave Macmillan.

Maisuria, A. (2014) 'The neo-liberalisation policy agenda and its consequences for education in England: A focus on resistance now and possibilities for the future', *Policy Futures in Education*, 12(2), pp. 286–296.

Maisuria, A. (2015) Margaret Thatcher's legacy, academisation and the demise of state education. *British Education Research Association (BERA) Blog.*

Maisuria, A. (2017a) 'Mystification of production and feasibility of alternatives social class inequality and education', In Cole, M. (ed.) *Education, Equality and Human Rights*, 4th ed, pp. 301–319. London, UK: Routledge.

Maisuria, A. (2017b) *Class Consciousness and Education in Sweden: A Marxist Analysis of Revolution in a Social Democracy.* London, UK: Routledge.

Maisuria, A. (December 2018) 'Neoliberal development and struggle against it: The importance of social class, mystification and feasibility', *AULA ABIERTA*, 47(4), pp. 433–440. Special Issue: Training for Critical Thinking and Social Commitment, University of Oviedo, Spain.

Maisuria, A., Cole, M. (2017) 'The neoliberalisation of higher education in England: An alternatives is possible', *Policy Futures in Education*, 15(3), pp. 602–619.

Maisuria, A. (2019) *England's school system is in crisis – could labour's national education service be the solution?* The Conversation. Published Feb 29th 2019.

Malott, C., Ford, D.R. (2015) 'Contributions to a Marxist critical pedagogy of becoming/centring the critique of the gotha programme: Part one', *Journal for Critical Education Policy Studies*, 12(3), pp. 104–129.

Marginson, S. (1994) 'The problem of 'transferable' skills', *Critical Studies in Education*, 35(1), pp. 4–28.

Marginson, S. (2019) 'Limitations of human capital theory', *Studies in Higher Education*, 44(2), pp. 287–301.

References

Marsh, S. (2017) *Suicide is at record level among students at UK universities, study finds*. Available at: www.theguardian.com/education/2017/sep/02/suicide-record-level-students-uk-universities-study (Accessed: 23 August 2018).
Marx, K., Engels, F. (2015) *The Communist Manifesto*. Milton Keynes, UK: Penguin Random House UK.
Marx, K. (2013) *Capital*. Hertfordshire, UK: Wandsworth Editions Limited.
Marx, K. (2014) *Economic and Philosophical Manuscript*. London, UK: Bloomsbury.
McAlpine, L. (2012) 'Academic work and careers: Relocation, relocation, relocation', *Higher Education Quarterly*, 66(2), pp. 174–188.
McLachlan, F. (2017) 'Being critical: An account of an early career academic working within and against neoliberalism', *Sport, Education and Society*, 22(1), pp. 58–72.
McLaren, P. (2015) *Pedagogy of Insurrection: From Resurrection to Revolution*. New York, NY: Peter Lang.
McLaren, P., Farahmandpur, R. (2001) 'Teaching against globalization and the new imperialism: Toward a revolutionary pedagogy', *Journal of Teacher Education*, 52(2), pp. 136–150.
McLaren, P., Martin, G., Farahmandpur, R., Jaramillo, N. (Winter 2004) 'Teaching in and against the Empire: Critical pedagogy as revolutionary praxis', *Teacher Education Quaterly*, 31(1), pp. 131–153.
Meranze, M. (2015) 'Humanities out of joint', *American Historical Review*, 120(4), pp. 1311–1326.
Monk, S., McKay, L. (2017) 'Developing identity and agency as an early career academic: Lessons from Alice', *International Journal for Academic Development*, 22(3), pp. 223–230.
Moore, P. (2009) 'UK education, employability, and everyday life', *Journal for Critical Education Policy Studies*, 7(1), pp. 243–274.
More, T. (2002) *Utopia*. Cambridge, UK: Cambridge University Press.
Morrish, L. (2017) *Why the audit culture made me quit*. Available at: www.timeshighereducation.com/features/why-audit-culture-made-me-quit (Accessed: 15 August 2018).
Nash, R. (1990) 'Bourdieu on education and social and cultural reproduction', *British Journal of Sociology of Education*, 11(4), pp. 431–447.
Neary, M., Saunders, G. (2016) 'Student as producer and the politics of abolition: Making a new form of dissident institution?', *Critical Education*, 7(5), pp. 1–23.
Nussbaum, M. (2010) *Not for Profit: Why Democracy Needs the Humanities*. Princeton, NJ: Princeton University Press.
O'Brien, T., Guiney, D. (2019) 'Staff wellbeing in higher education: A research study for education support partnership', *Education Support Partnership*. Available at: www.educationsupportpartnership.org.uk/sites/default/files/staff_wellbeing_he_research.pdf (Accessed: 15 June 2019).
Olssen, M., Peters, M. (2005) 'Neoliberalism, higher education and the knowledge economy: From the free market to knowledge capitalism', *Journal of Education Policy*, 20(3), pp. 313–345.
Organisation for Economic Co-Operation and Development (2002) *Education Policy Analysis*. Paris: OECD.

References

Osborne, G. (2013) *Chancellor George Osborne's autumn statement 2013 speech*. Available at: www.gov.uk/government/speeches/chancellor-george-osbornes-autumn-statement-2013-speech (Accessed: 20 August 2018).

O'Dwyer, S. (2016) *This (Un)certain life*. Available at: https://researchthatcares.com/2016/03/13/this-uncertain-life/ (Accessed: 5 August 2018).

O'Dwyer, S., Pinto, S., McDonough, S. (2018) 'Self-care for academics: A poetic invitation to reflect and resist', *Reflective Practice*, 19(2), pp. 243–249.

Ofsted (2019) *Summerhill school*. Available at: https://reports.ofsted.gov.uk/provider/23/103854 (Accessed: 5 June 2019).

Parr, C. (2014) *Imperial College professor Stefan Grimm 'was given grant income target'*. Available at: www.timeshighereducation.com/news/imperial-college-professor-stefan-grimm-was-given-grant-income-target/2017369.article (Accessed: 28 August 2018).

Parr, C. (2015) *Stefan Grimm death prompts questions for Imperial president*. Available at: www.timeshighereducation.com/news/stefan-grimm-death-prompts-questions-for-imperial-president/2019747.article (Accessed: 28 August 2018).

Peck, J., Tickell, A. (2002) 'Neoliberalizing space', *Antipode*, 34(3), pp. 380–404.

Pereira, M.M. (2016) 'Struggling within and beyond the performative university: Articulating activism and work in an "academia without walls"', *Women's Studies International Forum*, 45, pp. 100–110.

Petrina, S., Ross, E.W. (2014) 'Critical university studies: Workplace, milestones, crossroads, respect, truth', *Workplace*, 23, pp. 62–72.

Porschitz, E.T., Smircich, L., Calás, M.B. (2016) 'Drafting "foot soldiers": The social organization of the war for talent', *Management Learning*, 47(3), pp. 343–360.

Ratner, C. (2012) *Cooperation, Community, and Co-Ops in a Global Era*. New York, NY: Springer.

Research England (2018) *2018–19 grant tables for HEIs*. Available at: https://re.ukri.org/finance/annual-funding-allocations/2018-19-grant-tables-for-heis/ (Accessed: 23 May 2019).

Rikowski, G. (2012) *Life in the higher sausage factory*. Available at: www.flowideas.co.uk/?page=articles&sub=Life%20in%20the%20Higher%20Sausage%20Factory (Accessed: 12 April 2018).

Rikowski, G. (2017) 'Privatisation in education and commodity forms', *Journal for Critical Education Policy Studies*, 15(3), pp. 29–56.

Rizvi, S., Donnelly, K., Barber, M. (2013) *An avalanche is coming: Higher education and the revolution ahead*. Available at: www.ippr.org/publications/an-avalanche-is-coming-higher-education-and-the-revolution-ahead (Accessed: 28 August 2018).

Roberts, S. (Spring 2017) 'Introduction: Teaching critical university studies', *Radical Teacher*, 108, pp. 1–4.

Royal Holloway UCU (no date) *RHUL suspends UCU branch equalities and diversity officer*. Available at: https://royalhollowayucu.wordpress.com/2018/04/24/rhul-suspends-ucu-branch-equalities-and-diversity-officer/ (Accessed: 28 August 2018).

References 83

Rustin, M. (2016) 'The neoliberal university and its alternatives', *Soundings*, 63, pp. 147–170.
Ryan, H. (2017) *Educational Justice, Teaching and Organizing against the Corporate Juggernaut*. New York, NY: Monthly Review Press.
Saccaro, M. (2014) *Professors on food stamps: The shocking true story of academia in 2014*. Available at: www.salon.com/2014/09/21/professors_on_food_stamps_the_shocking_true_story_of_academia_in_2014/ (Accessed: 4 August 2018).
Saunders, D. (2007) 'The impact of neoliberalism on college students', *Journal of College and Character*, 8(5), pp. 1–9.
Sklar, H. (1980) Overview, in Sklar, H. (ed.) *Trilateralism: The Trilateral Commission and Elite Planning for World Management*, pp. 1–58. Montreal, Canada: Black Rose Books.
Smith, J. (2017) 'Target-setting, early-career academic identities and the measurement culture of UK higher education', *Higher Education Research & Development*, 36(3), pp. 597–611.
Smith, N. (2000) 'Afterword: Who rules this sausage factory?', *Antipode*, 32(3), pp. 330–339.
Social Science Centre (2019) *Social science centre farewell statement*. Available at: https://socialsciencecentre.wordpress.com/ (Accessed: 2 June 2019).
Srnicek, N., Williams, A. (2015) *Inventing the Future: Postcapitalism and a World without Work*. London, UK: Verso.
Summerhill (no date) *A.S. Neill's summerhill*. Available at: www.summerhillschool.co.uk/summerhills-fight.php (Accessed: 28 August 2018).
Sutherland, K., Taylor, L. (2011) 'The development of identity, agency and community in the early stages of the academic career', *International Journal for Academic Development*, 16(3), pp. 183–186.
Sutton, P. (2017) 'Lost souls? The demoralization of academic labour in the measured university', *Higher Education Research & Development*, 36(3), pp. 625–636.
The Equality Trust (2019) *The spirit level*. Available at: www.equalitytrust.org.uk/resources/the-spirit-level (Accessed: 28 August 2018).
The University of Utopia (2015) *Anti-curricula: A course of action*. Available at: www.universityofutopia.org/sharing (Accessed: 28 August 2018).
University and College Union (2016) *UCU wins recognition for precarious workers in the Coventry University Group*. Available at: www.ucu.org.uk/article/8432/UCU-wins-recognition-for-precarious-workers-in-the-Coventry-University-Group (Accessed: 20 August 2018).
University and College Union (2018a) *UCU announces 14 strike dates at 61 universities in pensions row*. Available at: www.ucu.org.uk/article/9242/UCU-announces-14-strike-dates-at-61-universities-in-pensions-row (Accessed: 20 August 2018).
University and College Union (2018b) *UCU agrees recognition deal with Coventry University Group*. Available at: www.ucu.org.uk/article/9487/UCU-agrees-recognition-deal-with-Coventry-University-Group (Accessed: 20 August 2018).
University of Exeter (no date) *About us: The Russell group*. Available at: www.exeter.ac.uk/about/facts/russellgroup/ (Accessed: 26 August 2018).

University of Oxford (2018a) *Oxford to benefit from government funding for research commercialisation*. Available at: www.ox.ac.uk/news/2018-04-11-oxford-benefit-government-funding-research-commercialisation (Accessed: 26 August 2018).
University of Oxford (2018b) *What have UG and PG leavers done 6 months after Oxford? Salaries distribution*. Available at: https://public.tableau.com/views/UniversityofOxford-DLHESurvey/Salaries?%3Aembed=y&%3Adisplay_count=yes&%3AshowTabs=y&%3AshowVizHome=no (Accessed: 27 August 2018).
University of Sheffield (2018) *Tuition fees*. Available at: www.sheffield.ac.uk/international/enquiry/money/tuitionfees (Accessed: 20 August 2018).
Ward, K., Wolf-Wendel, L. (2004) 'Academic motherhood: Managing complex roles in research universities', *The Review of Higher Education*, 27, pp. 233–257.
Weale, S. (2018a) *Bristol University faces growing anger after student suicides*. Available at: www.theguardian.com/education/2018/may/26/bristol-university-faces-growing-anger-after-student-suicides (Accessed: 23 August 2018).
Weale, S. (2018b) *Student mental health must be top priority – universities minister*. Available at: www.theguardian.com/education/2018/jun/28/student-mental-health-must-be-top-priority-universities-minister (Accessed: 23 August 2018).
Webb, D. (2018) 'Bolt-holes and breathing spaces in the system: On forms of academic resistance (or, can the university be a site of utopian possibility?)', *Review of Education, Pedagogy, and Cultural Studies*, 40(2), pp. 96–118.
Wolf, A. (2002) *Does Education Matter? Myths about Education and Economic Growth*. London, UK: Penguin.
Woodcock, J. (2018) 'Digital labour in the university: Understanding the transformations of academic work in the UK', *TripleC*, 16(1), pp. 129–142.
Wrigley, T. (2012) 'Class culture: Sources of confusion in educational sociology', *Journal for Critical Education Policy Studies*, 10(3), pp. 144–183.
Wyse, D., Torrance, H. (2009) 'The development and consequences of national curriculum assessment for primary education in England', *Educational Research*, 52(2), pp. 213–228.
Zajda, J., Rust, V. (2016) *Globalisation and Higher Education Reforms*. Switzerland: Springer International Publishing AG Switzerland.
Zajda, J. (2018) *Globalisation and Education Reforms: Paradigms and Ideologies*. Dordrecht, The Netherlands: Springer Science-Business Media B.V.
Zalewska, A. (2018) *University lecturer explains why academics are striking over pension cuts*. Available at: http://theconversation.com/university-lecturer-explains-why-academics-are-striking-over-pension-cuts-93039 (Accessed: 20 August 2018).
Zhou, N. (2017) *Calls for regulation of universities partnering with military-linked foreign companies*. Available at: www.theguardian.com/australia-news/2017/dec/16/calls-for-regulation-of-universities-partnering-with-military-linked-foreign-companies (Accessed: 20 August 2018).

Index

academic capitalism 40, 42
academic identity 45–7
Academics Anonymous 23, 40
Acker, S. 50, 51
Adams, J. 18
Allen, M. 9
Amsler, S. 19, 37
audit culture 17, 24

Ball, S.J. 24, 46
Becker, G. 10
Beckmann, A. 31
Benjamin, W 64
Bolsmann, C. 19
Bowles, S. 3, 6, 28
Bristow, A. 47, 50

Calás, M.B. 17, 30, 40
Cameron, D. 13
Canaan, J. 27–8
Capitalism: commodities production 3; *Communist Manifesto* 6, 15; equality 1; globalisation 7; human capital 3; imperialism 2; individualism 5; labour market 2, 4; labour power 1, 2; surplus value 1, 2, 6
Cleaver, H. 3
cognitive dissonance 28, 38; *see also* mental health
Cole, M. 9
collaboration 5, 32
collectivism 5, 26, 32, 61, 62
collegiality 5, 26, 32, 45, 56
commodification 3, 9, 16, 22, 55

Communist Manifesto, The 6, 15, 26
comradeship 5
Co-operative University 68–70; Social Science Centre 63–5; *see also* national education service (NES)
Cooper, C. 31
Critical Management Studies 47
critical pedagogy 65, public pedagogy 65; revolutionary critical pedagogy 65, critical reflectivity 33, 36; Student as Producer 64; student-teacher dichotomy 65
critical reflectivity 33, 36
Critical University Studies (CUS) 52
curriculum: skills and competencies 17, 47; classroom ethos 9; competition 30; content 30, 33; economic production 33; reforms 31; employability 30; neoliberal economy 32; bureaucracy 31; transferable skills 36

degree-level jobs 58
demand-side economics 10
Donoghue, F. 33

early career academics (ECAs): academic identity 45–7; complicity 47; ethical dilemmas 45; disillusionment 49; graduate teaching assistants (GTAs) 34, 35; performativity 46; power dynamics 49; *see also* PhD Students;
economy: economic productivity 19; growth 8; income inequality 9;

inequality 6, 53; underemployment 8; unemployment 8; wealth distribution 9
Eddy, P.L. 48
Engels, F. 1, 2, 6, 15, 29
entrepreneurialism 29, 30
employability 15, 29, 30
Evans, G. 20

Fazackerley, A. 38–9
feudalism 1–2
Fisher, M. 29
Freedom of Information (FoI) 56
Fulcher, J. 25
Furedi, F. 20

Gaston-Gayles, J.L. 48
Geoghegan, P. 27
Gill, R. 16
Gintis, H. 3, 6, 28
Giroux, H.A. 31–2, 71
global economy 34, 36
globalisation 7
graduate teaching assistants (GTAs) 34, 35; see also PhD students; Early Career Academics
Gramsci, A. 4, 53
Green, F. 5
Green Paper (2015) 60, 58
Grossi, G. 22

Hall, R. 24, 28–30, 32, 35
Hanson, S. 65, 68
Hatcher, T. 25
health: anxiety 35, 38, 41; Education Support Partnership (ESP) 39; mental health 27, 30, 38, 41, 42, 62, physical health 27, 30
Hegemony 5, 53; see also Gramsci, A.
Hill, D. 4, 5, 31
human capital 9, 11, 42; see also knowledge economy; labour power
humanities and social sciences 37, 38, 47

individualism 5, 39
Institute for Fiscal Studies (IFS) 20
International Co-operative Association 55
Isomöttönen, V. 48

Jaeger, E.L. 4

Kallio, K. 22
Kallio, T.J. 22
Keynesianism 7
knowledge economy: business product 11; educational qualifications 13; human capital 11; investment 12, 13, 19; labour force 14; labour power 13; social mobility 11; White Paper (2016) 12
Koukal, D.R. 37
Kynaston, D. 5

Labour Party Manifesto (2017) 54; see also National Education Service
labour power 1, 2, 4, 9, 11–14, 19, 24, 26, 24, 27, 34, 37
Loick, D. 47

McDonough, S. 32, 62
Macfarlane, B. 46, 56
McKay, L. 49, 50
McLachlan, F. 47–9
McLaren, P. 5, 65, 71
Maisuria, A. 9, 63
Marginson, S. 36, 37
marketisation 15, 43, 54, 60, 67
Marx, K. 1–3, 2, 6, 12, 15, 22, 34, 64
mental health 27, 30, 35, 38, 39, 41, 42, 62, physical health 27, 30; see also health
Meranze, M. 37
metrics 58
Monk, S. 49, 50
Mont Pèlerin Society 7, 8
Moore, P. 28, 31
Morrish, L. 41

national education service (NES): commodification 55; Co-operative University 68–70; critical pedagogy 65; cultural production 66; governance 56, 70; Labour Party Manifesto (2017) 54; national funding 61; Nolan Committee 55; popular education 65; professional autonomy 61; social and welfare services 64; Social Science Centre 63–5, 67, 68, 70;

social transformation 64; Teaching Excellence Framework 58
National Student Survey (NSS) 22, 58
Neary, M. 63, 64, 67
neoliberalisation 53: academic labour 27; *Academics Anonymous* 23; academics element 25; audit culture 17; cognitive dissonance 28; academic freedom 26; consumer/customer demands 22; competitiveness 16; economic productivity 19; employability 29; entrepreneurialism 29; financialisation 15; government funding 21; IFS 20, 21; individualism 16; laissez-faire approach 20; marketisation 15; NSS 22; performance culture 16; privatisation 16; proletarianisation 16; research commercialization 18; Research Excellence Framework 17, 22, 26; teaching and learning 15; teaching excellence 16, 22; Teaching Excellence Framework 22
neoliberalism: academic capitalism 40, 42; academic labour 34; *Academics Anonymous* 40; cognitive dissonance 38; financialisation 43; global economy 34, 36; human capital 9, 10, 42; individualism 39; Keynesianism 7; labour and productivity creation 8–11; labour market 37; labour workforce 8; marketisation 43; Mont Pèlerin Society 7, 8; NES 53; new and prospective academics 34, 36; performance targets 39; proletarianisation 34; student-as-consumer model 43; *see also* Mental Health
Nussbaum, M. 33, 36, 37

O'Dwyer, S. 29–30, 32, 62
Olssen, M. 7

Peck, J. 8
pedagogy 65, 40; public pedagogy 65; revolutionary critical pedagogy 65, critical reflectivity 33, "Student as Producer" model 64; student-teacher dichotomy 65; *see also* performativity
Pereira, M.M. 32
performativity 16–17, 22, 24, 25, 60
Peters, M. 7
PhD students 34, 35; graduate teaching assistants (GTAs) 34, 35; *see also* Early Career Academics
Pinto, S. 32, 62
Porschitz, E.T. 40
Pratt, A. 16
privatisation 16, 19, 40; *see also* neoliberalism
proletarianisation 16, 34; *see also* early career academics (ECAs)

Ratle, O. 47, 50
Reagan, R1, 7, 8
Research Excellence Framework (REF) 17, 22, 26; *see also* neoliberalism; metrics
Rikowski, G. 3, 22, 43
Roberts, S. 52
Robinson, S. 47, 50
Rustin, M. 52

Saccaro, M. 30
Saunders, D. 42
Saunders, G. 63, 64, 67
Smircich, L. 17, 30, 40
Smith, J. 47
Smyth, K. 30, 32
Social Science Centre (SSC) 63–5, 67, 68, 70
Solidarity 26, 41, 44; *see also* collectivism and collegiality
student-as-consumer model 43
"Student as Producer" model 64
surplus value 1, 2, 6

Teaching Excellence Framework (TEF) 22, 58; *see also* neoliberalism; metrics
technology: audit culture 24; British industrialism 25; capitalist system 23; cost-saving 24, 26; deprofessionalisation 23; digital learning strategies 24; 'lecture capture' 24; Massive Open Online Course initiatives (MOOC) 24; surveillance 24

Thatcher, M 1, 5, 7, 8, 13
Trade Unionism 13, 57; 44 Education Support Partnership (ESP) 39; *see also* University and College Union (UCU)

University and College Union (UCU) 44; *see also* Trade Unionism

Ward, K. 48
Weale, S. 42
Webb, D. 42, 52
Webber, M. 50, 51
White Paper (2016) 12
Wolf-Wendel, L. 48
work-life balance 45
Wrigley, T. 4

For Product Safety Concerns and Information please contact our EU representative GPSR@taylorandfrancis.com
Taylor & Francis Verlag GmbH, Kaufingerstraße 24, 80331 München, Germany

www.ingramcontent.com/pod-product-compliance
Lightning Source LLC
Chambersburg PA
CBHW051757230426
43670CB00012B/2323